Let My People
GROW

Tim Massengale

Let My People

GROW

A STORY OF CHURCH GROWTH

Let My People Grow

by Tim Massengale

©1989 Word Aflame Press
Hazelwood, MO 63042-2299
Reprint History: 1995, 1998

Cover Design Tim Agnew

Cover Art by Art Kirchhoff

All Scripture quotations in this book are from the King James Version of the Bible unless otherwise identified.

Printed in United States of America.

Printed by

 WORD AFLAME PRESS
8855 DUNN ROAD
HAZELWOOD, MO 63042-2299

Library of Congress Cataloging-in-Publication Data

Massengale, Tim.
    Let my people grow! : a story of church growth / by Tim
Massengale.
        p.   cm.
    Bibliography: p.
    ISBN 0-932581-41-2 :
    1. Church growth.   I. Title.
BV652.25.M2 1989
254'.5—dc19   88-31269
                                          CIP

To
my
loving and
understanding
wife,
Linda,
without whose patience
and help
this book would never have
been published

Contents

Figures

Foreword

Having had the honor of being Brother Massengale's pastor for a time and then having him as my full-time assistant, I know the heart from which this story came. He is a very enthusiastic, dedicated, and spiritual man. If you are hungry for progress in your local church, I am sure that within the pages of this book you will find many answers that you have been looking for.

It is one thing to *read* a book; it is another thing to pick up the *spirit* of the book. If you will pick up the spirit of this book and put into practice its principles with consistency, your church will grow—and growth is the will of God. The Bible says, "The Lord *added* to the church daily."

May you read this book and grow!

Vaughn R. Morton, Pastor
Truth Tabernacle
Fresno, California

Chapter One

How It All Began

The late afternoon sun filtered softly through the drawn, coarsely woven drapes, casting a faint lattice pattern on the carpet in the darkened study. An elderly man dressed in gray knelt in prayer beside an aged leather sofa. His gnarled hands clasped a worn, tattered Bible tenderly to his breast. Slowly he rocked his frail shoulders back and forth, moaning softly to himself. His nearly bald head, covered with but a few stray wisps of ivory-yellow hair combed back over the smooth, age-spotted skin, was bowed in deep supplication. Age lay visibly upon him. Deep wrinkles in his neck and face crossed one upon another, like multiple lines on a three-dimensional map, and were accented all the more by his tightly closed eyes and tense, drawn lips.

After a time, he raised his head and sighed, blowing his nose softly on a tear-dampened handkerchief. "Dear Jesus. . . ," he whispered as he rose carefully from the floor. He steadied himself upon the sofa's arm.

It was Sunday afternoon, the Lord's Day, and a time exceedingly special to him since Bonnie, his wife of fifty-one years, had unexpectedly died. Though several years had passed, her memory lived with him continually. For years they had knelt beside this same leather sofa and read their Bibles together. Then, hand in hand, they would pray before taking their Sunday afternoon nap. He still continued this time of devotion faithfully, and every time he prayed beside that sofa, he oddly felt that she knelt there too. At such times his heart yearned to see her again, to take her hand, to hear her sing, to see her playful smile. He often thought, maybe it won't be long now until I too can go home to be with the Lord.

But this afternoon had been strangely different. He shook his head slowly in wonder. The power of God had come so suddenly, so forcefully, almost as if the Lord had been waiting for him. As soon as he had knelt to worship, a tremendous burden had seized him. A feeling knotted deep within his soul, moving him to weep for over an hour in intercession. Even now, with the weight somewhat lifted, the powerful presence of God remained heavy upon him.

It was impossible to deny the impression he felt, and he was no stranger to the voice and impression of God. The Holy Ghost had spoken to him urgently about a young man whom he didn't really know and had seen only once. With the clarity of a vision he had remembered the young man—tall, slender, and well-spoken—who had stood before them that day, his words earnest and imploring. Though almost five years had passed, the old pastor could see him as if it were yesterday.

With youthful zeal, the young minister had come to see the district board. He sought their approval to start a home missions work in a small town where the truth had never been proclaimed. The old man, a presbyter then, had helped review the young preacher's application. He could still see the sincere look and hear the eager words washed with excitement as the preacher had made his impassioned plea. Yet now, for the life of him, he couldn't recall where the town was. Vaguely he remembered it being somewhere down south.

The old man shook his head again, his voice but a murmur. "Lord, how in the world am I going to find him? I can't even remember his name." Frowning with concentration, he wiped the beads of perspiration from his forehead and face. The voice of God had spoken clearly: the young man needed encouragement. But more than just encouragement, he needed help. He needed help now.

The old man studied the district directory lying open on the desk, his face reflecting his frustration. He had already searched it carefully without result. Name after name he pondered, trying to stimulate his stubborn memory, but more than a few were unfamiliar. It could be one of several dozen. Since the elderly pastor's retirement four years earlier, many new churches had been started, most by men he had never met.

He was not able to travel much now, not since a mild heart attack had taken his strength. His extended convalescence had left him largely out of touch with district matters. This, too, was a source of great sadness.

The elderly man glanced at the old regulator clock ticking softly upon his desk. It was 4:00 P.M. Evening service started in a few hours. "Lord," he prayed aloud again, this time his voice breaking with emotion, "I've done all I can do. It's in Your hands now. But if You'll somehow let me know who he is, I'll . . . I'll do the best

13

I can."

As he moved slowly toward his desk to sit down, tears flooded his eyes once more, and a feeling of quiet expectancy swept over him. The Spirit of the Lord was still very, very near.

Where Would It End?

The irritating ring of the telephone sharply interrupted Pastor Steve Martin's thoughts as he leaned back in his broken-down desk chair in the cheaply panelled church office. It was Sunday afternoon, and the little building sat wrapped in silence. Steve had closed his eyes only moments before, hoping to lessen the headache that threatened to develop behind his temples. Pastor Martin had been getting a lot of headaches lately.

"Springville U.P.C.," he intoned, grabbing the receiver on the second ring. "Yes, Brother Rick. How you doing? . . . I'm sorry, brother. Yes, I knew you were waiting to see me this morning, but I had a counseling problem arise . . . no, that's all right, I knew you would understand."

Pastor Martin listened a moment longer, then sat forward abruptly. "What? . . . You're kidding!" Shock registered plainly in his eyes as he listened to the caller on the other end. "Where? . . . You . . . you have no other options?" Slowly he rubbed his temples and forehead. The headache was now in full swing.

"Now, Rick, this type of decision is pretty serious. You don't want to jump too quickly. Yes . . . yes, but hold on a minute. Let's pray about this first. You know how badly we need you here." His brow drew together in a worried frown. "Now . . . now, Rick, . . . No, I feel you are dead wrong . . . No, you have done a fine job so far. It's just a little slow getting started . . . Okay . . . Well, we're going to believe something will turn up . . . Of course I'll pray . . . All right . . . Well, I'll talk with you tonight . . . Okay . . . 'Bye."

With an audible groan, Steve lowered the phone from his ear. "Not the Myers family, Lord," he wailed softly. He gazed at the wall distractedly as the full implications of the phone call began to sink in. Slowly he dropped his head down onto his arms on top of the desk.

The Myers family were among Pastor Martin's first converts when he came to the small, picturesque town of Springville in the southeastern part of the state five years ago. Rick and Ann were also his most faithful, supportive saints—as fine a family as he would ever hope to meet—and deeply involved in every part of the infant country church. But now Rick, a welder at the local electrical plant, was being transferred—and ironically, he was being transferred to Texas!

Pastor Steve Martin had come from Texas five years before to start the little home missions work in Springville. He was much younger then, only twenty-two years old. But with his tall, six-foot-four frame and broad, heavy shoulders, he looked considerably older. He combed his thick, tawny-gold hair back from his wide forehead. The profile of his face was sharp and confident. He had a strong, aquiline nose and a mouth that was ready to smile. His quick wit and bold personality had done much to win over the townsfolk. In a crowd, his presence was compelling. But apparently looks and personality were not enough.

Pastor Steve Martin had put five hard years of sweat,

labor, and prayer into making the church what it was to-day. The church had come to birth in revival—the explosive type of revival that kept the altars filled with seekers and the baptismal waters fresh and clean. The first two years saw the budding assembly grow to about seventy—good by anyone's standards—and it looked as if they would soon outgrow their facilities.

However, the last couple of years hadn't gone as well. The church appeared to come to a numerical standstill. Months had passed without anyone new in the altar. Then they lost several families—and God knows they had precious few to lose—because of job situations. They began to struggle financially. Only recently he had had trouble with yet another couple. Now that couple was sullen and distant, attending only occasionally. Before, each day had held promise, but now it seemed to hold only problems.

As if he were far older than his twenty-seven years, Steve slowly pushed back his broken chair and stood up. I just can't believe this is happening, he thought. Why does it all seem to happen at the same time? Why can't something go right for once? Am I doing something wrong?

He walked away from the desk, his wide shoulders slumping forward and his stomach aching with the inner pain of tension and fear.

At the window he gazed out at the church's gravel parking lot. Across the street a large apartment complex was in the early stages of construction. The stark, unfinished studs and beams formed a skeletal structure against the gray, cloudy sky. For the last several months he had watched the construction workers scurry like so many bees on a hive: digging and pouring the foundation, cutting and setting the block, bending and clamping the plumbing.

Now, as he studied it absent-mindedly, he could see that the framework was practically complete. He reflected upon the many mornings he had walked over to study each phase painstakingly, picturing and dreaming how the same steps would apply to building a new sanctuary on the six acres east of town—six acres that had embodied his future dreams of growth and revival.

In a bold act of faith, his handful of members had stepped out three years ago and purchased property just across the town line on the old main highway. Back then, it had seemed like a dream come true. He had negotiated a surprisingly good price. It required very little down and had low starting payments. The payments, the bank had explained, were to increase slowly until the loan was paid off. At the time, this type of arrangement did not trouble him. The church had been in consistent and steady revival. He figured the increased financial burden would be easily offset by the growth of the church. After all, there was some risk in anything. And this risk appeared small considering the forward thrust they had seen.

But in the last two years, his cherished dream of a new facility had begun to dim. The payments were becoming increasingly difficult because the church was only a little larger now than when they had bought the property.

Oh, it wasn't as if they hadn't seen folks saved. They had. But every time it looked as if they would break the one-hundred mark, something would happen—transfers, deaths, backsliding, folks moving for first one reason then another—and now this. Rick Myers was his youth leader, and his wife taught the junior girls in Sunday school. They both were good soul winners. Two families had come to the Lord by their witness, and one family, the McFarlins, were still good members today. What if Rick couldn't forestall the transfer? How could he ever hope to replace the faith and support they provided?

Then, suddenly, another thought struck him. Brother Marker—he had forgotten about him! Two weeks ago, Brother Marker, his longstanding Sunday school superintendent, had asked to talk privately. Sitting in Steve's office, he dropped the bombshell: he was resigning his position. Pastor Martin had shaken his head in disbelief as he heard Brother Marker lamely claim that he didn't have time to do the position justice. "And besides," the older man had said sadly, "nothin' I ever done worked like much anyway." Every argument Steve could think of had fallen on deaf ears. The white-haired gentleman had sat quietly, eyes cast down, shaking his head in resignation, and refusing to be persuaded otherwise.

First the Sunday school, now the youth—where would it end?

"God, Why Have You Failed Me?"

Turning abruptly from the window, Steve walked over to the office door and entered the tiny sanctuary. A quick glance took in the unpretentious house of worship. The church had been here for four years. It wasn't much by the world's standards, but Steve always felt that God had given it to them.

They rented it from the big Baptist church uptown. Many years before it had been the original Baptist church location. The land upon which the simple brick building sat had been willed to the Baptists many years before, but under strict conditions. The requirements of the deed stated that, first, it must remain a church and, second, it must never be sold. If either condition was broken, it would revert to the former owners. So the Baptists rented it—one office, four small Sunday school rooms, and a sanctuary with hand-built pine pews. It was clean, neat, and attractive in a country sort of way, but with pitiably little room to grow.

"Grow! What a joke," Steve muttered disgustedly to himself. "Everything I do turns to sour apples."

Suddenly it all began to wash over him—the work, the effort, the time, the labor. Everything appeared to be falling apart slowly. Not just Sunday school and youth—he could live with that—but so many other plans and programs had failed. It seemed that he climbed over one brick wall only to find another. Hope fell into failure, excitement turned into discouragement. Dreams crumbled into disillusionment and eventually became barren sands of disappointment and despair.

"Why even try to get back up?" he mumbled bitterly. "I'll only be knocked back down."

Suddenly, without warning, tears flooded Steve's eyes. Blindly, he groped his way down the aisle to the front of the church and dropped down at the same altar where he had prayed with countless others. He tried desperately to pray, his whitened fists clenched tightly upon the altar before him, but he felt as if God were a million miles away. A great swelling, choking pain tightened within his throat and chest, a pain that finally burst forth into a loud and painful sob.

"O, God! O, God, why?" he cried out over and over again.

19

Steve wept. Great convulsive sobs rocked his shoulders and body. He wept for what must have been hours, tortuous tears forming small, glistening pools upon the hard, polished wood. He reminded God of all the sacrifices he had made just to come here, the hours of labor he had spent, and the seeds of truth he had sown. He looked back over the past few months—twice on extended fasts, entire days in prayer. All the while he had but one motive in mind: revival. His soul longed for, hungered for, revival. Many a night he had gone to bed only to climb out again and find a place of prayer to weep over his city.

Now he was angry. He was hurt. He felt that God had let him down. "I've done my part, God," he sobbed brokenly, "why haven't You done Yours? They told me that if I did my best, You would do the rest. What's happened, God? How come it's not working? Why have You failed me?"

Questions were followed closely by accusations as self-pity threatened to grip him in its stranglehold of bitterness. With head bowed and face buried, he poured out his pent-up feelings onto the smooth pine slab.

Later the words of David in Psalm 142 would come to him: "I cried unto the LORD with my voice. . . . I poured out my complaint before him; I shewed before him my trouble. . . . My spirit was overwhelmed within me." Unlike Job, Steve could not say that he "charged not God foolishly," for that is exactly what he did.

But as the fountain of pain flowed from his eyes, the bitterness born of disappointment began to crumble and fade. With each sob, with every tear, the burden lay increasingly upon the altar. The Holy Ghost, with the unexplainable peace that is beyond understanding, slowly began to minister to his defeated, demoralized heart.

But then, it had always been so. God had always been there when Steve Martin needed Him—comforting, encouraging, uplifting. He knew the foolishness of his accusations. God was not at fault for these problems. The Lord cared more about his church than anyone. After all, it wasn't "his" church, but it was "His" church—it belonged to the Lord. These were His people. This was His building. It was all His.

Never Again the Same

Abruptly the spirit of Steve's prayer began to change. No longer was he asking God why, but rather what. "What, Lord, would You have me do? Where do I go from here? What do you wish of your servant next?"

With the change of attitude came a change of spirit. A tremendous weight slowly lifted from his heart, and with its departure a wonderful presence swept gently over him.

Later, in looking back upon that Sunday afternoon, it was difficult for Steve to explain exactly what had happened. A vision? He wasn't sure. A dream? He couldn't say. All he could be sure of was the voice of God speaking patiently, tenderly, and vividly clear. He heard tender words, yet at the same time, intense words—words that were to change the entire course of his ministry. Never again would he be the same, for the message would forever burn like fire within:

My son, I hear your cry. I know the troubling of your heart, your sorrow, and your pain. I see your disappointed and lamenting soul. But hear My voice. Be at peace, be calm.

21

Though you weep for all that could have been, for hopes and visions that now will never be, know that I am not a God of the past. Let the broken dreams fade as though they never were, for it was not My will that they should come to pass.

You are My child, My servant, the one I have chosen to lead My people. As you follow Me, so they will follow you. My sheep know My voice, for I am their shepherd. Do not trouble yourself, and weep no more, for I am with you. Nor will I ever forsake you.

Know that this moment is the dividing line of your life. To this place I have carefully brought you. Broken, I can remold you. Crushed, I can remake you. This is My will. What is past is dead. Let the dead bury the dead. Follow me.

Do you not know that many have trodden this path of trial and disappointment? Do you not know that I have led many through discouragement and pain? I have shown them the way of victory and understanding. As I have shown them, so will I show you. Hearken to my words. Listen closely as I speak. I desire to teach you and lead you. You still have much to learn.

Seek now those of the hoary head and the weakened step. Though they be of many years and their eyes be dimmed, yet their understanding is great. With age has come wisdom. With experience has come understanding. I have taught them, and now they will teach you. Hear their words as though they were My own.

Now go. Choose him to whom I have spoken. I have prepared him as I have prepared you. Seek the one who spoke so boldly to your heart in the message you were given two weeks ago, for he is a servant precious in My sight.

He will teach you the answer to your questions and instruct you with experience and learning. Hearken to him, for with his counsel you will prevail.

As the Lord spoke softly and kindly to Steve's heart, the hardness began to weaken and pale, so that long after the voice of God had faded, he continued to pray, resting in the overwhelming sweetness he found.

When Steve arose from the altar that day, the late afternoon sun cast long silhouettes upon the auditorium's hardwood floor. Somehow he knew with an inner assurance that this time it would be different. God had heard his prayer; the answer now would come. How? He did not know. But the promise was unquestionably his. Nothing would ever make him doubt what the Lord had said. He embraced it tightly within his heart as a beggar clutches a gold coin.

He drew in a deep breath and let it out slowly, stretching his cramped legs and feet. After wiping his eyes with his handkerchief, he looked at his watch; it was almost 4:00 P.M. If he was going to make a long-distance phone call, he would have to hurry. And call he would, for the words of the Lord were still vivid and fresh in his mind: *"Choose him to whom I have spoken. I have prepared him as I have prepared you. Seek the one who spoke so boldly to your heart in the message you were given two weeks ago, for he is a servant precious in My sight."*

Two weeks previously, sitting in his office, Steve had eagerly listened to a tape that a fellow pastor had loaned him. The message had been delivered at a sectional ministers conference up north several months before. His friend had mentioned the name of the speaker, but Steve promptly forgot it, never having heard of the fellow before. The tape label was blank, except for the title, and the title had captured his attention. In bold letters was written "LET MY PEOPLE GROW." He had smiled at the play on words taken from God's famous command to Moses.

The speaker turned out to be tremendous. From the timbre of his voice, Steve could tell the man was elderly. Yet the strength of his speech disclosed an excitement and enthusiasm rare for someone that age. His message was powerful. He spoke of revival and growth with the firsthand knowledge of those who had experienced it. Woven throughout his message were many excellent suggestions for leading a church into revival, particularly in the areas of management and motivating people. Several outreach methods also sounded promising. But the part that had spoken most strongly to Steve's heart was a simple statement given in closing.

"To help your church grow," the old man had said, "it is not necessary that you know everything about church growth. It is only necessary that you know what is important. I have found several irrefutable laws—principles, if you will—in God's Word that are pivotal keys. These keys are the simple truths that unlock the doors of faith and growth. When applied, they always work, for God's Word can never fail."

The speaker had gone on to list several basic and fundamental principles that surprised Steve with their simplicity, yet stirred him with their accuracy. However, these particular points, twelve of them in all, had only been mentioned in passing.[1] Much to Steve's disappointment, he had not elaborated or expounded on any of them.

Steve recalled thinking that if he could only grasp these concepts, and then find a way to apply them, he might have the answers he had been praying for. It was then he had purposed to ask his preacher friend who the speaker was and possibly find some way to talk to him. Now the Lord had told him to do exactly that. He was absolutely sure of it.

Steve quickly walked to his study, this time flipping on the fluorescent lights as he entered. The tape, he remembered, was still in the small cassette player that he kept on his desk. Reaching over, he ejected the tape and examined it more closely.

He groaned in disappointment. He had been afraid of that. The tape and label were store-bought. The title had been simply written by hand, and that was all—no name, no location, nothing. He then glanced at the back. "Sectional Conference—Ellisburg" was neatly printed, along with a date of several months before.

"Well, at least that's something," Steve told himself.

Ellisburg, he remembered, was about three hours north. But then, it was probably only the church where the message was preached. Most likely the preacher was from out of town, perhaps even from out of state. He scowled at the tape in frustration. How could he find out the preacher's name? How was he going to get in touch with him? Then he remembered. Of course. He could call the neighboring pastor who gave him the tape. Surely he would know. And his pastor friend should still be home.

Five minutes later he set the phone down triumphantly, breathing a sigh of relief. He had a name! It was a fellow by the name of Keller, and he was from Ellisburg. He had a good-sized church, too—over six hundred—so

25

he must be doing something right.

He hurriedly scanned the listings in the district directory until he saw the city: "Ellisburg Apostolic Tabernacle, Tommy Keller, Pastor." The feeling that swept over him as he read the name was impossible to describe. With pounding heart he realized that this was the person God had told him to seek out. This was the "servant precious in My sight" who would show him what to do, or perhaps even what he was doing wrong.

He frowned slightly at the name. "Tommy Keller," he whispered softly. He had never heard of him, which was not surprising. In the five years Steve had been in the state, his job had hindered him from going to any district meetings. He had not been raised in church, and he knew few pastors outside his own section. He had never seen or heard of many well-known preachers mentioned by his friends. Though he had evangelized a short while, it had mostly been in Texas. Coming from a small church and attending only a handful of conferences had left him totally out of touch as far as his fellow pastors were concerned.

His hand trembled slightly as he dialed the number. He had no idea what kind of response he would get. After all, it wasn't every day that God said to call someone.

"Apostolic Tabernacle," a strong male voice answered on the second ring. "Pastor Keller speaking."

"Brother Keller," Steve blurted, his voice sounding funny to himself as he spoke, "my . . . my name is Steve Martin and I'm the pastor of the United Pentecostal Church in Springville, south of you. You don't know me, sir, but today I was praying and. . . ," Steve swallowed the nervous lump rising in his throat and rushed hurriedly on, "and I felt the Lord impress me to call you about a message you preached several months ago. It was called 'Let My People Grow.' I felt that you might . . . uh . . . might be able to answer some questions I've been struggling with, and I thought if you had some time, I might talk—I mean, we might get together, and . . ."

Steve trailed off, suddenly feeling foolish for rambling on as he had. His palms suddenly were sweaty.

The phone was silent for several uncomfortable moments. The voice then answered in a very slow and deliberate tone. "I'm sorry, Pastor Martin, but I'm afraid you are mistaken."

Steve's heart shattered. "But . . . but isn't this Pastor Keller?"

"Yes, it is, but you have the wrong man. I'm sorry, but the Lord didn't tell you to talk to me!"

Chapter Two

"How Badly Do You Want to Grow?"

As Steve hastily backed his battered, green '78 Buick out of the driveway, he waved to his wife, Judy, a final time before accelerating rapidly down the quiet residential street. His mind was too preoccupied to notice the deep azure blue of the sky, the tall, billowing fullness of the clouds, or the crisp freshness of the November morning. His tires squealed as he made the sharp right turn onto the northbound freeway ramp, leaving a black cloud of exhaust as he floored the accelerator. He was clearly in a hurry.

Jockeying quickly onto the busy interstate, he scowled accusingly at the innocent clock on the dashboard before him. It read 9:25 A.M. He was late. That meant it would be after 12:00 before he arrived in Ellisburg. He had wanted to arrive before noon and had awakened early for just that reason. His packing had taken longer than he had anticipated, however. Two suitcases now lay in the back seat, bulging not only with clothes, but with church

29

records, program outlines, notebooks, and whatever else he thought he might need. He wasn't exactly sure what he would be doing or how long he would be staying. Two or three days, anyway, is what Elder Keller had said.

He smiled faintly as he remembered the telephone call the day before. "You have the wrong man," Tommy Keller told him bluntly. "I didn't preach that message. My father did. He's retired now, although you'd hardly know it by the way he acts. You're welcome to call him. Yet let me caution you: his health is poor, so he doesn't get out much. He used to visit churches to preach and help them with growth and organization and stuff like what you heard on the tape. Unfortunately, he's unable to do that anymore. But if you want to talk to him, I'm sure he would be glad to answer any questions you might have. But remember, Brother Martin, church growth is his sugar stick, so be careful that he doesn't run you up a hundred-dollar phone bill. Here, let me give you his number."

Remembering the next phone call sent dozens of tiny chill bumps up and down Steve's back all over again.

He had called the second number, and after introducing himself to Elder Jeremiah Keller, the old man simply cut him off. "So you're the one," he said softly, his raspy voice edged with excitement. "God be praised. I've been sitting here for over an hour waiting for you to call."

Before Steve could ask him what he meant, the old pastor asked what town he pastored in and what year he had started. After Steve told him, Elder Keller briefly recounted his prayer meeting and what the Lord had told him. When the old man finished talking, Steve wept afresh. He could hardly talk except to get directions.

"I feel," the elderly pastor said, his deep southern accent coming through faintly, "that the Lord wants you to spend a few days with me as a guest in my home. God impressed several things on my heart that you need to hear. I know everything isn't going just as you want it to, son. Don't worry; the Lord knows all about it. He's a way maker."

Feeling the joy and thrill of coming face to face with the supernatural, Steve prayed for another hour after that phone call. A tremendous thankfulness and gratitude swelled within him. To realize that God cared enough to put him and Elder Keller together and speak in such a persuasive way to them both at the same time—oh, the wonder of it all! Never before had Steve felt such assurance that God would send revival to Springville.

Only Three Voting Members

Steve turned off the freeway and drove into town. Ellisburg claimed a population of about forty-five thousand. It was typical of most towns in the state, having one, long main street carrying the majority of business. Various other streets, lined with banks, gas stations, variety stores, supermarkets, drug stores, and so on, branched off the main one. Steve went directly through the center of town, past the post office, courthouse, and city hall.

He followed the winding avenue out of town just as Elder Keller had directed. At the flashing, yellow caution light he took a right and stayed on the thickly wooded lane until it came to a dead end. Turning right again, he began to watch for the mailbox number. He passed it up once before finally spying it among several others.

31

A dirt road, replete with potholes large enough to scrape his bumpers, led him back into the tall poplars and stately pines that grew in a thick tangle on either side.

Breaking through the trees, he came to a clearing with an enormous, neatly trimmed lawn. A wide circular drive bordered with squat, low-lying shrubs followed the line of foliage before angling to the left in front of the house.

The house sat toward the back of the clearing, an older, two-story brick home with a broad country porch wrapped from front to back. Tall picture windows lined the face and sides, interspersed with smaller latticed ones and looking like so many embattlements upon a rustic fort wall. White shutters framed the windows and matched the white doors and trim. Two massive chimneys stood like towering soldiers on either side of the house, one with a faint trail of smoke wafting toward the sky. The general appearance reminded Steve of the old farmhouse his grandparents used to own in Georgia—sort of southern colonial without the pillars. He liked it.

As Steve drove up to the porch and parked, the front door slowly opened and an elderly gentleman stood framed in the doorway. Steve guessed his age to be around seventy-five, although he could have been older. He stood with his thin shoulders slightly bent. A bright smile spread upon a face touched heavily by years, yet it was the radiant kindness in his eyes that reached out and touched Steve. If he had any previous apprehension, it quickly faded at the warmth and sparkle that came from the seasoned man of God.

"Greetings, my friend," Jeremiah Keller called, his strong, raspy voice resonant in the crisp chill of the

November morning.

"Praise the Lord, sir," replied Steve as he climbed out of the car.

No other words were uttered, nor were any needed, as the old man walked slowly down the flagstone steps and clasped Steve's hand and neck in a tight, surprisingly robust embrace.

"It's good for you to come."

"Thank you, sir, for inviting me. I hope I'm not intruding."

"Intruding? No, no, young man. Martin isn't it? No, Brother Martin, you're not intruding at all. With my wife gone, it gets somewhat lonesome out here with nothing but crickets and bullfrogs for company. No, son, I'm looking forward to talking with you. You and I are going to get along fine. I feel it in the Holy Ghost. But come, let's not stand in the cold. Let me help you with your bags."

Elder Keller took the small overnight case and led the way up the steps and into the large, double-door entry. An old, multicolored basset, whose ears dragged on the carpet of the entry hall, greeted them as they came through the door. The gray-muzzled hound looked up at Steve with big, liquid-brown eyes, its tail wagging experimentally. Steve reached down to pat his head and quickly withdrew, surprised by a soft growl as the dog sniffed curiously at his pant leg.

Elder Keller laughed. "Don't let ol' Lazarus frighten you. He's unaccustomed to visitors. He couldn't bite you because he has no teeth to speak of." Then the old man's eyes twinkled. "You can't always tell, though. He might try to gum you a bit!"

Steve grinned broadly. "Lazarus?"

"Yep. He sleeps so much of the time that I can't tell whether he's dead or alive."

Chuckling, Steve knelt down and coached the old dog into letting him scratch behind his long, floppy ears. Lazarus promptly rolled over to have his belly rubbed.

"Ha!" the old man laughed. "See there, he likes you, and any friend of Lazarus is a friend of mine."

Steve stood up and surveyed the room beyond the arched entry. The large living room flickered with the warm, yellow light provided by a brisk, crackling fire in the broad, gray-stone fireplace. A thick, wooden mantel crowned the hearth, on which sat a beautiful handmade, four-masted, model sailing ship.

On either side of the mantle, covering the wall from ceiling to floor, stood two hardwood bookcases, filled to overflowing with volumes of leather-bound books, dusty and cracked with age. An old, overstuffed floral sofa and matching easy chair sat on one side of the room with a brass, floor reading lamp and glass coffee table. To one side of the sofa and closer to the entry stood an antique upright piano also lined with books across the top.

A tall, straight-backed rocking chair sat in the far corner, its seat and back padded with hand-quilted pillows. The opposite wall opened into a dining room, with the kitchen beyond. The house reminded Steve of the old Currier and Ives lithographs he had seen when he was a child. The simple warmth and informal atmosphere beckoned to him. He inhaled deeply.

Elder Keller led the way into the room, which smelled faintly of burning wood and cedar panelling. "You eaten yet?" he asked, one gray, bushy eyebrow cocked in a question.

"No, sir," Steve replied, "but I grabbed a cup of coffee and doughnut as I left this morning, so I'm not hurting."

"Then, here, let me show you to your room upstairs. I'll make us some sandwiches. It's almost lunch time. I don't know about you, but I'm starving."

After depositing his bags in his room, Steve sat at the kitchen table and watched Elder Keller fix lunch. The kitchen was much like the rest of the house, looking like an early 1920s or 30s *Good Housekeeping* cover. The cupboards were handmade and painted neatly in soft cadmium gold. The curtains over the deep porcelain sink were country ruffle, checkered yellow to match the tablecloth and place mats. So far, the only thing modern about the entire house was an electric range beside the sink and a new double-door refrigerator on the far wall, both of which looked entirely out of place. From the latter, Elder Keller was busy getting sandwich fixings and placing them on the counter.

"Tell me," Steve asked after they had exchanged the normal small talk, "have you been retired long?"

The older man, carefully slicing an enormous ruby tomato, replied without looking up. "About five years. My wife passed away a year before that. I guess it was stress that prompted a minor heart attack. Nothing serious, but it drained my strength and forced retirement. My son, whom you talked to already, pastored up in Kentucky then. The church invited him to come when I announced my resignation."

"How long did you pastor here?"

"Nineteen years."

"Did you start the church?"

35

"Nope."

Elder Keller set the platter of ham and turkey sandwiches on the table and poured two tall glasses of milk.

"I came here in '64 to take the church—that is, what was left of it. We had only three voting members then. Of course, that's not saying much, because the first year two of them died and the third moved away."

Steve laughed. "No kidding? So you basically started with nothing?"

"Well, we had a tiny building that was little better than a storefront. The church had been somewhat larger many years before I came, averaging in the eighties, I think. However, when the sawmill closed down, several families moved away. Then the church went through several pastors that did little more than collect tithes . . . and of course, there were other hornets in the nest. But the Lord called me to Ellisburg to build a church, not take one. I'm thankful for how He's blessed us."

"How's the church doing now?" Steve asked.

"Good. As I said, the Lord's blessed us. The Sunday school averaged about 780 this last month. We're running well over 500 on Sunday night. About six . . . no, seven years ago, we built a completely new facility on ten acres north of town. It seats around 600. My son, Tommy, is making plans to build a new sanctuary beside the old one now."

"Boy, that sounds exciting." Steve's voice was filled with admiration. "How many will your new building seat?"

"We had the sanctuary plans designed to be built in three stages. The first stage will seat 800 on the ground level. Later, by moving one wall, it can be expanded to

1,000. Finally, a balcony will add another 300."

Steve looked puzzled. "Why not do it all at once? Too expensive right now?"

"Nope. Tommy and I both kinda like a church to always look about half full. It's depressing to walk into a church that's almost empty. This way, we expand in steps. Each new addition gives the congregation a new vision of growth . . . and more room to shout, too," he added with a wry smile. "We really believe in worship. But listen, Brother Martin, tell me . . ."

Steve broke in. "Please, Brother Keller, call me Steve."

The old pastor helped himself to another half of a sandwich, liberally spreading it first with hot mustard relish. "All right, Steve, but enough about myself. Tell me about you and your church. That's what's important right now. You didn't drive all this way to talk about our new building."

"I Feel Like Such a Failure"

Steve drank the last of his milk and leaned back with a sigh. "Well, it all started five years ago when I was traveling as an evangelist in Texas. I got a call from Brother Townson in Logansport—that's just north of Springville—to come preach a revival. I passed through Springville on my way to Logansport, and right off the town spoke to me. You know what I mean? It wasn't a voice or anything, yet it reached out and touched my wife and me.

"The town was so clean and quiet. It sat back off the main highway and was bordered on three sides by rolling hills. All the homes and yards were so neat and well

37

kept. It looked like something out of a post card somewhere. It was so strange, yet even then we felt that we belonged there."

Steve leaned back in his chair, his eyes staring out the window with a faraway look as he remembered. He sighed once again, then looked back at Elder Keller and continued.

"Anyway, when we stopped to get a bite to eat, the people displayed such an open friendliness that it surprised us. I began talking to a waitress at the cafe, asking her what church she attended and things. Somehow we began talking about the Lord, and boy, was she hungry for God. She had just gone through a divorce, and her life was all messed up. I told her about home Bible study, and she said she'd love one—just like that! When I asked her the location of the United Pentecostal Church in town, she told me she didn't know of any church by that name. I couldn't believe it, so I checked the phone book—nothing listed. The ministerial directory showed nothing either. The closest church was Logansport, the town where I was preaching the revival, and that was seventeen miles away.

"Well, to make a long story short, my wife and I ended up teaching her a Bible study on the off night of the revival. Then one evening she drove to Logansport for the services and received the Holy Ghost. We baptized her that same night. Her sister and her ex-husband also came to the Lord and later a cousin. In all, nine people received the Holy Ghost from Springville during that revival. Yet sadly, they had no church to attend. That's when I appealed to the district board for approval to start a new work."

Elder Keller slowly nodded his head. "Yes, I was

there. I can remember you telling that to the board. And
you've been there how long?"

"Five years this coming February. God blessed the
first two years, and we saw wonderful growth. We
averaged forty at the end of the first year and about sixty-
five by the end of the second. But these last two or three
years . . ." Steve paused, then shook his head. "I don't
know what's wrong, Brother Keller. Nothing seems to
work. We've grown close to a hundred a few times, yet
we always seem to start losing folks. Problems would
come up, people would start moving, some would backslide. Seemed like first one thing, then another . . ." Steve
shrugged. "We've been averaging about seventy now for
the last three years."

"Hmm . . ." the older pastor chewed on his lower lip
thoughtfully. "Tell me about your outreach."

"Well, right now it's pretty sparse. Yet I think I've
tried just about everything there is to try. Home Bible
studies have worked better than anything, I guess.
However, it's hard getting anyone to teach them besides
my wife and me. When I taught the studies, they did fine.
The problem is, I work almost full time painting houses
for a contractor in town. The income of the church isn't
enough by itself, so I divide what little time is left between
prayer, study, sermon preparation, counseling, visitation,
and keeping the church clean and repaired. I try to take
a day each week to be with my family, although I don't
always get it. When the church averaged less, I had more
time to teach Bible studies. Now that it's larger," he
spread his hands regretfully, "it's hard to get any evenings free."

"Are any of your saints teaching Bible studies now?"

"Not that I know of."

"Are *you* teaching a Bible study now?"

"No . . . ah . . . not right now."

"I see. What else are you doing?"

"Well, I bought a bus after we were there about a year. I had a couple of young people who expressed interest in getting a route started. That also went fine when I did it myself. We brought in thirty to forty children, and our attendance averages really jumped. After several contests we pumped up our average close to a hundred. But then the teachers started to complain that they couldn't control that many children—they said they felt like babysitters—so after a while the excitement and interest died down. After that, a personal problem arose that kept me from working the route on Saturday. I gave the responsibility to one of my young men, but for some reason it slowly died. Now the bus is just sitting behind the church collecting rust."

"That's too bad. Anything else?"

"Well, we knocked on doors to invite folks to church. In fact, in our second year, we divided the town into sections and knocked on every door in the city limits. It took us months, working every Saturday. We all got calluses on our knuckles. We found contacts for home Bible studies, bus ministry, Sunday school enrollment, and callback visitation. That brought some results.

"We've also passed out thousands of tracts, hitting shopping centers and parking lots. We've held street meetings, park services, and rest-home services, and we've run newspaper ads . . ." Steve paused to consider, then continued, "I even rented a billboard once. And, of course, we've had revivals. Everything we did worked to some extent, I guess. However, nothing brought the results I anticipated.

"I mean, don't get me wrong, I don't regret any of it. We've seen a bunch of folks saved. In fact, I baptized a young man just a few months ago . . ." Steve frowned then and shook his head sadly. "But folks just don't stick anymore. They get the Holy Ghost, I baptize them, and they do just great for two or three months. But then some problem comes up, and the next thing you know, they've backslidden and won't talk to you any more. I'm at the place now that I don't know what to do."

Steve's wide shoulders slumped dejectedly forward, both arms propping up his chin, discouragement written plainly over his face. "You know what, Brother Keller? I really feel like a failure. I went to Springville with such high hopes to build a church, my heart charged with faith. Yet now—" Steve made a futile gesture with his hand. "I guess I've completely blown it. Nothing I do makes any difference." He sat for a moment in silence, eyes downcast.

Outside somewhere a sparrow sang softly. Off in the distance a dog began to bark. The young pastor heard none of it, lost within his thoughts, drifting in the deep waters of despondency. He finally glanced up at the elderly man sitting silently across from him, his eyes imploring, his voice urgent.

"I'm serious, Elder, you're my last hope!"

Disappointed or Discouraged?

Elder Keller sat quietly, staring solemnly at the young man from beneath deep, bushy eyebrows. He said nothing for so long that Steve wondered if he was going to reply or not. Then, ever so slowly, the old man leaned forward, his hands flat on the table before him, until he was almost standing up. He gazed intently at the young man until Steve shifted uncomfortably. Yet curiously, he was unable to look away. Finally, the old pastor spoke with carefully chosen words.

"You've made two statements, Steve, that give me cause for concern. Let me ask you something. You said you were discouraged. Are you really discouraged? Or are you just disappointed?"

Steve frowned, stammering with confusion. "I . . . I'm not sure what you mean."

"The difference, young man, between discouragement and disappointment is vast. Discouragement makes you want to quit, to give up. It means you're completely defeated. But disappointment doesn't mean defeat. Disappointment doesn't make you want to quit. Instead, Steve, it makes you want to change! To do better! So why did you come here, son? To tell me you want to give up? If so, you might as well leave this old man right now. Or do you really want to know how to do better? Are you really willing to change?"

Steve stared at the elderly pastor, surprised at the intensity in his voice and the harshness of his words. He knew Elder Keller wasn't playing games. He also knew that his entire future could well depend upon his answer. When he finally replied, his voice murmured low and deliberate.

"I'm not a quitter, sir. God promised me revival in my city, and I intend to have it. Furthermore, I'm willing to do whatever has to be done to obtain it. I came here for you to show me how."

The old man nodded his head as if that settled a major issue. He leaned back with a sigh, the relief showing plainly in his eyes. "All right, Steve. Now, you also said you feel like a failure. There's no shame in failing, only in quitting. Failure is not always bad, and many times it can be good. The only person who never fails is the person who does nothing. If we learn by our mistakes, we will be that much wiser when we meet that problem again. The trick is to find out what caused your mistake and to correct it. Tell me, son, to what would you attribute your failure? What's the cause?"

Steve scowled again. He wasn't sure that he liked this quizzing game. He let his mind reflect on the past few years, on everything he had done and gone through. He considered his people, the trouble he had had with the Johnson family and how they had pulled out the Tolburns when they had left. He saw Brother Corrie, the young man he had asked to assist him, and how that had ended in such disappointment and hurt feelings. He contemplated his little building, so inadequate for a growing congregation. He saw the miserly educational facilities, the leaking roof, the baptistry that had to be pumped out by hand, the difficulties imposed by renting.

He looked at the financial burden, the strain that the new property had placed upon the church, the sad lack of tithes and offerings, which forced them to spend much of their energies in fund raising just to pay the mortgage and rent. Not only that, he had to work—often on Saturdays—and that divided his time so much. The size of his little town . . . people's indifference . . . so many things contributed to the situation. But when he finally answered, he knew without a doubt the true reason. It wasn't an easy thing to say. He took a deep breath and let it out slowly.

"Elder, I guess the main problem, when you truly come right down to it, is me. I could point my finger at many, because a lot of things have gone wrong. I could sit here all night and give you enough to fill up a book. But my dad always told me that blaming others never solved anything. It's just an escape. If something doesn't work, it's my fault. To blame something or someone else is to avoid the real issue. He was quite fond of that old saying 'The buck stops here,' and I guess that's probably as true in my case as anything."

As Steve finished speaking the old man's face was shining and his smile was kind and understanding. He looked like a father whose son had just gotten a perfect report card. "Son," he said, his voice husky, "you don't know how glad I am to hear you say that. Your father's a smart man. You see, it makes what I've got to say a whole lot easier.

"A fellow doesn't drown by falling into water; he drowns by staying there. The Lord sent you to me for help. I feel that I can help you, or I wouldn't have wasted my time asking you to come. Your recognition that you need help, and being man enough to admit it, is half the battle.

"I've tried to help a lot of pastors. Many want me to share with them the principles that the Lord has given me. However, when they pointed the finger of blame at their people, or their facilities, or their location, or their having to work, or a dozen other reasons that I've heard through the years, there was nothing I could do to help. When some 'body' or some 'thing' has made you fail, then you're sure as shootin' right, you are a failure."

The young man looked dubious. "Why is that?"

"Because the solution to your problem is completely out of your hands. You and I cannot control people or circumstances. They do and happen of their own accord. The only thing you can control is yourself. So if the real problem is yourself, then the power to change lies within your grasp.

"The Apostle Paul put it this way. He said, 'I can do all things through Christ.' The key words in that passage are *I* and *Christ*. Paul realized that his ability to succeed rested in his personal dependence on the power of God. If things went well spiritually, it was because he had faith in God. His faith released the power that accomplished the task. Yet if things didn't go well spiritually, the same held true. He wasn't trusting in God to do the work."

The young man scratched his head thoughtfully, then with a suddenly knitted brow he asked, "But what if it simply wasn't God's will for it to happen?"

"Some things fall into that category, son, and in those situations it becomes important to seek God until you are sure of His will. But in most cases you already know His will. You see, Steve, you don't need to seek His will about praying each day or studying His Word. You already know the answer, because His Word plainly tells us to do this. By the same token, you don't need to ask God if it's His will for your church to grow. You already know it's His will to grow. This is the purpose and intent of the church. The heartbeat of Jesus Christ was to seek and save the lost. Since the church is the body of Christ, then we should manifest this same burden. Our number-one priority is always to see souls come to complete salvation, and if the

45

church is doing this, it will grow."

Thou shalt have unshakable faith that thy church will grow, for this is God's plan and purpose for His church.

Steve waved his hand impatiently. "I know it's the overall purpose of the church to grow, yet couldn't it be God's will for some men to pastor small churches? I mean, some preachers may be incapable of pastoring a church of a thousand."

"Steve, don't misunderstand me. I didn't say that a church must be large to be in the will of God. I said it must be growing. Growth must be the yardstick by which every church is measured, because growth denotes life. If the number of church members is not steadily increasing, it's not fulfilling the purpose for which God created it. You see, if a church is not growing, it's dying. A stagnant situation will never exist as far as the church is concerned. The body of Christ will advance or retreat—but it'll never stand still."

Steve held up his hand again, a suggestion of annoyance in his eyes. "Wait a minute. What do you mean by standing still? My church has pretty much stood still for the last three years. We're not growing, yet neither are we declining. Our number is consistent."

The old man nodded his head. "True, a pastor might

46

argue, 'My church has remained in the seventies or eighties for the last five years; it's standing still.' But I say, no, it's declining, because when a church ceases to grow, the revival spirit and vision are slowly fading. The longer a church goes with its altars barren of souls, the less faith it will have in its ability to conceive. This is true in the natural as well as the spiritual. Your numbers might not be dying, but your saints' vision for growth and revival is!

"You see, Steve," he continued, "growth is a fundamental trait of all living creatures. This is especially true of the church. Why, just look at the examples in the Bible to describe it: body, flock, vine, family, bride, and so on. The basic function of all these is to grow or reproduce. But the beautiful difference between the church and other forms of life is that it's not just a mortal body, it's also an eternal body. All natural life will eventually perish and decay, but the church will live on." The old pastor was leaning forward earnestly now, waving his arms excitedly to stress each point.

"The church is uniquely able to resurrect itself from the rubble of ruin. Like Israel of old, it can return from captivity and rebuild its walls, redig its wells, and reconstruct its temple."

He stabbed a bony finger in Steve's direction, eyes flashing, voice rising in volume. "But the choice is yours! Just as Nehemiah chose to rebuild, you can choose to grow. No congregation has reached its fullest potential. No pastor is too old to lead his church into constant revival. Why, just look at Moses. The age of the body, son, is not as important as the vision in the heart!" He concluded by bringing his fist down sharply on the table

47

for emphasis.

With that, Elder Keller leaned back and fit his fingers together on the table before him, as if to force himself to slow down and to be less ardent. Throughout this speech, Steve sat with his mouth hanging slightly open, too surprised at the old pastor's exuberance to do anything more than nod. The old pastor looked pleased with himself at the effect he was having upon the younger. After a few seconds he caught his breath and continued, his eyes twinkling.

"Now, about that pastor you say may be incapable of pastoring a church of a thousand. Son, you're looking at one. But in my situation, I never desired to try. When my church reached about four hundred on Sunday night several years back, I felt that, for me, it was big enough.

"Truth is, we could be running close to a thousand today, save for the fact that I took almost sixty families and used them to start five new churches around the Ellisburg area. We have daughter churches in Newburg, Shady Lake, Thomasville, Clovis, and Porter. One of them is running around two hundred right now.

"Yet keep in mind, son, that we never stopped growing and revival never ended. I just flat refused to let it. I'm convinced that a church is much like a bicycle: unless it's going forward at a brisk rate of speed, it wobbles; too sluggish, it falls over. Young man, if your church is going to grow, you've gotta do more than hope or believe it will grow, you gotta make it grow."

"Just How Badly Do You Want It?"

Steve had closed his mouth and was now chewing on his knuckle distractedly, slowly letting Elder Keller's words sink in. He knew that what the elderly preacher said embodied truth. He needed to hear every word.

It was not as if he hadn't heard it before. In fact, he had preached much the same to his church. Yet he needed to hear it from someone else—someone who had done it. And he realized that this was not just Elder Jeremiah Keller talking, but God was talking too. He was not surprised to feel the surging presence of the Lord sweep over him, reproving and convicting him for his poor attitude and vision.

When Steve finally spoke, the lump in his throat gave his voice a somewhat strangled tone. "What should I do, sir? How can I change? Where do I get that kind of faith? How can I get what you got?"

The old man stood to his feet and slowly began to clear the dishes from the table. "Let me tell you a story from my youth. Maybe it'll help.

"I was about your age when I first started evangelizing. It was different in those days. In the 1930s you traveled by bus—few could afford their own car—and lived out of a suitcase and carpetbag. Churches that stood for truth were distant and far between. At the end of your meeting, sometimes you were paid; more often you were just fed and given the bus fare to your next stop. The first year of travel I struggled something terrible. I didn't get many calls to preach. I can't recollect doing too much eating either. I often had to stop and work odd jobs just to live.

"That year at the district camp meeting, I met another evangelist who stayed extremely busy. He had a powerful ministry. Many souls received the Holy Ghost in his tent revivals, and miracles occurred in practically every service he preached. The demand for his ministry was so great that he had far more invitations than he could ever accept. I could not help looking in envy at his ministry and wondering if perhaps God was being partial. I longed to have a ministry such as his.

"One day, I began talking with him, and I got bold enough to ask him point-blank, 'Brother Jackson, how can I get what you've got? How can I develop a miracle ministry like yours?' I'll never forget his answer, it stirred me so.

"He looked me squarely in the eye and replied, 'How desperately do you want it? Are you willing to pay the same price that I paid? Are you willing to pray, and keep praying, until you get answers from heaven? Are you willing to fast until your ribs stand out like an old washboard? Are you willing to study and memorize the Word until it becomes a part of you, until it burns like holy fire within? Are you willing to separate yourself, be misunderstood, be ridiculed, be called a fanatic? To want a miracle ministry is a noble thing, my friend, but just how badly do you want it?' "

The old man paused, his eyes glistening with tears beneath the craggy brows. Carefully he reached over and placed his rugged, aged hand on the young man's shoulder. "So, Steve, how desperately do you want it? Are you willing to put forth the effort it will take to have a real move of God?" The old pastor's voice grew soft and intense. *"Just how badly do you want to grow?"*

The two men stared at one another for several seconds, neither saying a word. Then the elderly pastor turned back toward the counter and carefully began to stack the dishes in the sink. Steve slowly rose to his feet and walked from the room.

"Where you going, son?" Elder Keller called out as Steve was halfway across the living-room floor.

Steve paused but didn't turn around. His voice choked with emotion, he replied, "If you don't mind, sir, I feel that I need to pray. I think I'll go to my room for a while."

Chapter Three

Dreaming the
Impossible Dream

"More pie, son?" Elder Keller asked encouragingly. The supper dishes, along with what was left of the barbecued spare ribs, had already been removed from the table, and a sizable, deep-dish blackberry pie—almost half gone—sat between them. A nearly empty carton of old-fashioned Blue Bell ice cream gave evidence to the indulgence of their appetites. Steve wiped his mouth and sighed—a sound that was more like a groan.

"No, sir . . . uh . . . thank you anyway, but if I ate another bite I'd be sinning. That dinner was deliciously epicurean."

"Epicu . . . what?"

"Epicurean." Steve repeated. "Just another way of saying it was excellent. Did you make that pie, Elder?"

"Yep," he replied proudly. "My wife, Bonnie, used to make them like that before she died. Now there was a real cook."

"I'm sure, but you need to warn folks not to get any

of that pie on their forehead. That could be suicide."

"Huh? What do you mean? Why's that?"

" 'Cause if any landed on your forehead, your tongue would beat your brains out trying to get to it."

"Oh, go on!" Brother Keller scoffed, his mouth twitching with amusement, then finally breaking into a cackle in spite of himself. "Glad you liked it. Now, let me put this pie away, and we'll break out the checkers."

"Checkers?"

"Sure! You think I brought you all the way up here just to preach at you?"

"Well, I . . . uh . . ." Steve trailed off.

The old pastor grinned mischievously. He liked keeping the young man off balance. "Now go on into the living room. You'll find the checker box under the coffee table. I'll be there in a minute."

Steve, wondering briefly what he was getting himself into, went obediently into the half-lighted living room and sat down on the overstuffed sofa. After first turning on the brass reading lamp, he found the well-worn box where Brother Keller said. Taking out the red and black playing board, he had just begun to place the checkers in their proper places when something wet and cold touched his bare leg above his sock. He pulled back in surprise, cracking his knee painfully on the heavy glass coffee table and spilling game pieces on the floor.

"Ow!" Rubbing his bruised knee he looked down into the bright, coffee-colored eyes of Brother Keller's aging basset hound. "Lazarus," he said with mock distress, "you startled me. You need to warn people before you go sticking that cold nose of yours around." He gently scolded the old dog in an amused tone while reaching out to scratch under the gray-speckled muzzle and ears. Lazarus responded by breaking into a wide, doggy grin, his tongue hanging comically out one side of his mouth. To Steve, it looked as if the dog enjoyed the trick he had played. He patted the dog a final time and quickly retrieved the scattered pieces.

The Law of Accident

He had just finished setting up the game when the elderly preacher sat down across from him. "Best way I know to stimulate the mind," the older pastor stated in a matter-of-fact voice. He ran his hand absently over his nearly bald head. "A real game of strategy. You play much?"

"No, I'm more of a chess player myself." Steve hated to admit that he hadn't played checkers since grade school.

"That right? Well, then, you should be a fitting checker player, too. I've always preferred checkers myself. It's more like pastoring."

Steve glanced up, surprised. "Pastoring?"

"Sure! Pastoring and playing checkers have a lot in common."

Steve wrinkled his nose. "You're kidding me," he said. Checkers was not his favorite game. Maybe that was why he hadn't done well at pastoring either.

The old man grinned broadly. "Nope! I'm dead-eye serious. Look here. You've got two opposing forces, the black and the red. Your men, the black, represent the devil. Now, my men are red. I like to think they used to be black, but now they're covered by the blood of Jesus."

The young man leaned forward, resting his elbows

on his knees and began to chuckle, shaking his head in disbelief.

"Hold on," Brother Keller exclaimed, his face registering a mock seriousness. "I'm not through yet. You think I'm kidding, but I'm not."

Still grinning, Steve apologized. "I'm sorry, Elder. It's just that I've never heard this before."

The old man gave him a sly wink. "You'll hear a whole lot of new things before this week is over, son, if you keep your ears open. Now, let me finish. I'm the pastor and my blood-washed men represent my church. I have two main objectives in this game: the first is to capture as many of your men as possible and bring them over to my side; the second is to get as many of my men kinged as possible."

"What does getting your men kinged have to do with the church?"

"Doesn't the Bible say we are to reign with Christ as kings and priests? I'm going to capture as many of the devil's victims as I can. Then my goal is to get them all to the other end of the board to be crowned. You see, Steve, the reason that many churches don't grow is because the pastor doesn't truly understand the two main objectives of the church."

"Which are?"

"Which are just what I said—to convert the sinner and to present those converts pure and spotless before Christ. That's the reason for our existence. That's why the Lord gave the fivefold ministry: for the perfecting of the saints for the work of the ministry. The church's ministry is the same as Jesus had—to seek and save the lost."

"But . . . don't all pastors realize that?"

"Oh, I'm sure it's in the back of their mind somewhere. The problem is, their actions don't show it. Their priorities are all out of whack. For example, one pastor I talked to several years ago said, 'Boy, we're sure working hard.' 'Getting much done?' I asked. 'No,' he replied, 'just working hard.' "

Steve let out a snort of amusement. "I know what he's saying. I've felt the same way."

"Exactly. We have plenty of activity, yet little productivity. The devil would like to get all of our churches so busy that they can't win the lost. One important job for every pastor is to make sure the church stays focused on its objectives. Every activity, function, and ministry must be closely examined in the light of these two objectives. If we are entangled in anything that is not helping us fulfill our purpose for existence, we need to avoid it. You see, I'm a strong believer in the eighty-twenty rule."[1]

"Eight-twenty rule? What's that?"

"Well, it has many applications. But one is that eighty percent of your results come from twenty percent of your activities. One real key to growth, Steve, is to identify that twenty percent and let nothing take its place. If a Friday-night softball game means that the turnout for Saturday-morning visitation is poor, then the softball should go or be rescheduled. Many pastors have an acute case of the 'used to's.' When you ask them about home Bible study or bus ministry or visitor follow-up or door knocking, they will tell you that they used to do it, yet for some unknown reason it died.

"You read the Book of Acts, son, and you quickly find where the priorities of the Early Church lay. They evangelized in the marketplace, in homes, in synagogues, in jail, before rulers and kings, and everywhere throughout the city. The high priest proved the extent of their witness when he said, 'You have filled all Jerusalem with your doctrine.' "

The young man nodded thoughtfully. "I hate to admit it, Elder, but you're right on target as far as my church is concerned. You asked me earlier if I had much outreach going. I don't. I used to . . . however, I've allowed other things to take its place. Everybody is busy, but with the wrong things. It seems as if my people are doing anything and everything for the work of God except reaching the lost."

"Don't feel too bad, you have plenty of company. The Book of I Kings tells of a servant who was given the job of watching a prisoner during battle. The prisoner escaped. When the servant was asked to explain what happened, he said, 'While your servant was busy here and there, the man disappeared.' Notice: the servant was busy, but not doing what he was told to do. Tell me, son, what did Jesus tell us to do?"

The young man crossed his legs and leaned back. "Ouch. That hurts. It doesn't leave much excuse, does it?"

"No, it doesn't. Not for you or any other pastor. If your church doesn't have a strong outreach program, everything else should stop until you do. That's the number-one priority.

"Let me give you an example. I heard one of my Sunday school teachers testify once that during the winter about seventy percent of the bus kids would come to class with runny noses, so she would wipe them. Well, she discovered that that was about all she was doing—wiping little noses. She finally decided, I'm not here to see that they have clean noses. I'm here to teach them something unforgettable from the Word of God. So she taught them and let them drip!

"Paul said, 'All things are lawful unto me, but not all things are profitable.' In other words, there are many things I *could* do, but few things I *should* do. Hear me well, my friend: outreach is not an option."

The young man gazed out the window at the growing darkness, lost in thought. When he finally spoke, his voice revealed strong inner emotions. "But, sir, it wasn't my intention to let my outreach slip. I never consciously thought, I'll drop home Bible study. It just . . . seemed to happen. But since it happened once, how do I keep it from happening again?"

Outside, the wind whistled faintly over the chimney draft, causing an occasional finger of smoke from the fire to drift into the warm room. Lazarus twitched gently in his sleep as he lay curled before the flames.

The old man leaned forward, his voice again becoming intensely earnest. "Steve, listen carefully, for I don't want to be misunderstood. A church doesn't grow by accident; it grows by choice. Those who live by the law of accident—that what will be, will be, and nothing I do will change it—accomplish just that: nothing. That kind of attitude makes as much sense as saying that Roger Bannister was out jogging one day and accidentally broke the four-minute mile, or that Sir Edmond Hillary just took a casual stroll one evening and found himself on top of Mount Everest. No, Steve, those who achieve something in this life, or in the work of God, have a definite aim and purpose. Yet the opposite of that also holds true."

Dream the Impossible Dream

The young pastor stood suddenly and walked over to the broad picture window at the far end of the room. Here the room was heavy with shadows. He gazed out into the deepening twilight. A thin layer of clouds hid the stars over much of the sky. Only in a few places could he see the tiny pinpoints of light. When he finally answered, it was without turning around.

"So, what exactly do you propose that I do?" His voice sounded tense in the darkened stillness of the room.

"Son," Elder Keller replied in a soft, gentle tone, "great men of God never sought to be great. Glory was not their goal. They simply followed the vision that God had given them and did what had to be done. Success and growth will come, Steve, with the realization that you can't do everything *you* want to do, but rather, you must do everything *God* wants you to do."

The young man whirled around, his eyes and voice betraying his frustration. "But you sound as if I haven't tried—as if I've been playing church and twiddling my thumbs—when in reality I've poured my guts out. I've done everything I've known to do. Sir, you said on that tape that it's not necessary to know everything about church growth, only what's important. All right, tell me what's important. That's what I came here for. Do I have to get on my hands and knees? Brother Keller, I'm begging you. Please tell me what to do!"

"Young man," Elder Keller said, his voice still soft, "I'm trying to tell you. The reason you are so frustrated is because you have no clear sense of direction. You see, nothing is more discouraging than not knowing where you're going, because you never know when you get there.

60

Let me say that again. *Nothing is more discouraging than not knowing where you're going, because you never know when you get there.* What you need, Steve, is a clearly defined vision—and not only for this year, but for every year, and for the rest of your life.

Key Concept Two

**Thou shalt not wander aimlessly
but shalt have positive direction,
clear purpose, and definite goals.**

"Solomon said, 'Without a vision, the people perish.' That's your problem, son. Instead of a vision to look at, all you have are the daily problems of pastoring. No wonder you feel discouraged. You must lift your eyes off the problems and focus upon the vision that Jesus would have you to reach. You need to set some concrete goals."

The young man frowned, "You mean like Sunday school goals? I can't see where contests and stuff will help."

"I'm not talking about contest goals. I'm talking about growth goals. And not just number goals alone, but also quality improvement goals. You will never reach numerical goals without also implementing an improved program."

Then the old man smiled. "Now come over here and sit down and quit acting so hurt. We'll get nowhere this week if you take everything I say personally. I'm not talking about you alone but about pastors and churches in general." Then he paused, his eyes twinkling, "However, if the shoe fits, wear it."

The young man sighed and walked over to sit down. "I'm sorry, sir, for sounding sharp. It's just that I've tried so hard and nothing has worked. I can't help but feel that I've wasted these last three years."

"Oh no, son, they're not wasted, because now you know what not to do. I remember reading that Thomas Edison's assistant threw up his hands to quit after their eight hundredth experiment failed to produce a light bulb. 'No,' Edison said, 'the experiments are a success. Now I know eight hundred ways that won't work!'"

The young man smiled. "At least I'm a good bad example."

The old man chuckled. He reached back behind the sofa and withdrew a tablet of paper. "Now, let's set down some definite goals for you this next year."

Steve frowned. "Elder, I'm uneasy about this goal-setting business. Goal setting is a product of the positive mental attitude movement, and I've always felt that the PMA stuff had its foundation in humanism—only glorified self and flesh—so I've steered clear of it."

The old man grinned. "Let me tell you a secret, son. Those positive mental attitude folks stole their ideas from us. Much of what they teach has a strong Bible basis, even though it's often distorted. This Bible is the most positive book around. Here, let me show you. Take that," he gestured to the stout family Bible that lay on the coffee table, "and turn to Philippians 3:13." Steve did as he was told and Brother Keller continued.

"Paul said, 'This one thing I do.' That's goal setting. A goal is simply a fixed objective. He had taken the many activities of his life and narrowed them down to one central priority, aim, and passion. For goals to work they must be focused. Broad, general goals are worthless, because you never know when they are reached.

"For example, reaching my city with the gospel is a general goal. Having a big church, many new converts, or a nice sanctuary is much the same. The words *big* and *many* and *nice* sound good, but they are too general. They cannot be quantified. You have no specific number to reach. Now, seeing one hundred souls baptized this year is a true goal. It is specific in quantity. You know when you reach it. Are you following me?"

The young man nodded.

"Paul then went on, 'Forgetting those things which are behind.' This shows that he refused to dwell on past failures. He forgot the negative and concentrated on the positive. Those PMA folks that you mentioned are always talking about positive thinking. The idea of a positive mental attitude was nothing new to the early church. Paul asked the Romans, 'If God be for us, who can be against us?' That sounds pretty positive to me. The Bible also tells us to gird up the loins of our mind and bring every thought into obedience. That is what the PMA people are saying. They just take it out of a biblical context."

Steve nodded his head again without saying anything and motioned for the old pastor to continue.

"Paul then said, 'Reaching forth unto those things which are before, I press . . .' This shows that he had a burning, all-consuming desire. When it came to living for God and preaching the gospel he let nothing deter him. He reached, he pressed. Those are words of absolute determination.

"It amazes me to realize all that Paul achieved in his short life span, establishing dozens of churches and evangelizing most of Asia Minor. Do you realize he did this without a car, a printing press, a radio, or any of the other modern methods we often take for granted? What Paul did have was a burning desire, a total commitment to the work of God that would eventually drive him to declare, 'I am ready not to be bound only, but also to die . . . for the name of the Lord Jesus.'

"Steve, you must have that same kind of fervent desire, a desire that causes you to press on, to not give up. A church is like a fine musical instrument. It's tuned one string at a time. However, a piano that is only half tuned sounds no better than one completely off key. Once you start on this journey, don't give up. Don't let your dreams die. I have short- and long-range goals, but I also have life goals. These take longer. I may never reach them all, but I'll always keep trying. Fact is, your being here has helped me take another step toward one of my life goals."

"Really?" Steve responded in surprise, "What's that?"

"Almost ten years ago, I asked the Lord to let me teach these principles to fifty young men. You're number thirty-seven."

"You've done this thirty-seven times?"

"Yep. Of course, I used to go to a man's church and work with him there. I'm unable to do that now."

"My, that must be exciting to help a church to begin to grow. How are those thirty-seven pastors doing?"

"Well, some have ignored my suggestions. You see, not all who say they want to grow are willing to pay the price. However, those who have followed my guidelines have at least doubled, and most are still growing."

"Sounds good; keep talking!"

"Well, notice that Paul not only said he pressed, but he pressed 'toward the mark.' In other words, he aimed at something. Steve, you need a mark to aim at. You need to see the first step. Not only was there one thing Paul had a goal for, but he set step-by-step marks to evaluate his progress. The goal of one hundred converts this year can be broken into steps of eight converts per month. That way you can evaluate your progress every month. If you can't break the goal into bite-sized pieces or steps, it's not a true goal. Besides, one hundred converts looks hard; eight looks much easier."

The young man smiled. "Mile by mile, life's a trial—inch by inch, it's a cinch."

"Where'd you hear that?"

"My dad gave it to me on a plaque when I was a kid."

"It's true, son. An ample, growing church doesn't happen overnight. It is developed over a period of time. Finally, Paul said he reached 'for the prize of the high calling of God in Christ Jesus.' He set his priorities in the proper place—doing the Lord's will until His return. He knew that the will of God was his only goal and purpose in life.

"Why, son, every person in the Holy Book had a goal they strived for. Noah's goal was to build an ark. Abraham searched for a city whose builder and maker was God. Moses set his sights on delivering the Israelites. Joshua determined to conquer Canaan. David dreamed of a glorious temple. Nehemiah's goal was to rebuild the walls. Even God had as His ultimate goal the redemption of mankind—His goal was the Cross!''

The old preacher's voice began to take on an air of excitement. "You want a better word to use than *goal?* Faith! Faith is the substance of things hoped for, the evidence of things not seen. Faith sees the invisible, feels the intangible, and achieves the impossible. A goal is simply believing that what you don't have you can have. As long as your goals agree with God's will, nothing can hold you back."

With vibrant excitement, the old pastor began to wave his spindly arms in the air. "Why, when I get to thinking about what God has done for me and what he's fixin' to do, I get so excited I can hardly stand it. It makes me almost want to shout—in fact, I think I will!" And with that he stood up and did a careful, little two-step jig around the coffee table. Steve nearly fell over laughing at the sight of it.

The old man stopped in front of Steve, his arms spread wide. "Why shouldn't I shout? I set a goal of a church of four hundred, and God gave it to me. I set a goal of starting five new churches, and God helped me do it. Son, I challenge you to dream the impossible dream! God delights in achieving the impossible. Just remember," the old pastor paused, his face sobering slightly, "faith without works is dead. God refuses to do it by Himself. He could, but He won't. He expects us to do our part, too."

I'm Going to Do It

The young man sat back thoughtfully. "Dream the impossible dream! I like that. So you're saying I should just dream up a number and shoot for it."

"No," Elder Keller sat down, pointing at him with

a long, bony finger, "I didn't say that. I said you need to have clearly defined goals. You don't just pull it out of your head. God must put in in your heart. Nor should it be just a dream; you have to turn it into a goal."

"What's the difference?"

"A dream is not set within any time frame. It floats out in the future somewhere. A goal has a specific date by which it must be accomplished. You want to see one hundred souls baptized? Fine, but when? This year? Next year? Twenty years? It must be within a time frame to be a true goal."

"All right, when do we start?"

"Start what?"

"Setting goals. You've convinced me. How do I start?"

The old pastor leaned forward and flipped open the note pad. Licking the end of his pencil, he continued. "Goal setting starts with your dream, Steve, your vision—that vision that God has placed in your heart. Let me ask you a question. Think about it carefully. If everything goes well for your church for the next few years, what do you think your Sunday school average will be, let's say, five years from now? Now, before you answer, keep in mind your facilities and the time required to build. Be realistic, yet let your faith go. By realistic, I mean it can't be something totally out in left field. It must be—"

"Wait a second," the young man cut him off, "you said to let my faith go. Believe God for the impossible. Now you tell me to be realistic in my dreams. I don't get it."

"Steve, when I say realistic, I mean according to your

capabilities. You're only human—you can only do so much. You may be capable of pastoring a church of a thousand, but if the entire thousand dropped in your lap this year, you could never establish them. That's almost ninety people per month, and ninety new converts is a lot of babies.

"Son, here's the way I look at it. God wants to break every goal I set. If I set it at two hundred, God wants to give me three hundred. In other words, He wants to do above and beyond what I ask or think. So I'm going to set my goals at what I'm realistically capable of doing. Then, when God breaks that goal—which I'm confident He will do—He will get the glory, and that's what we want Him to get, don't you think?"

Steve smiled broadly. "You know, Brother Keller, you sure have a way with words."

The young man sat back in the soft cushions of the sofa, and for a full three minutes he was lost in thought. Then he spoke. "You know, Brother Keller, on the way up here I began to think back over the last five years. If we had continued to grow these last three years as we did the first two, we would be over three hundred today. I feel that God put that number in my heart several years ago. I know three hundred sounds adventuresome, but I have faith that God can give it to me."

"Are you positive?"

"I think so, sir. To be absolutely sure, I need to pray more about it."

"Do that. Goals set lightly are also lightly discarded. They must burn with intensity. Now, I want you to take the tablet, son, and write down your goal. Then, subtract your current Sunday school average to get a total."

The young man wrote:

```
300  five year attendance goal
-75  current Sunday school average
225  difference (growth goal)
```

"The 225," continued Brother Keller, "is the amount you need to grow in order to reach your five-year attendance goal. This is your *growth goal* for Sunday school. Now, most people would simply divide the 225 by five to get a goal for each year. If you divided that number by five, you would need to increase your average by forty-five each year. I'll tell you right now, that would be a difficult task for your little church this first year."

"I might be able to do it with a contest," Steve suggested.

"We're not interested in a one-shot number, son. We are looking at the average. What we're going to do, is place your growth goal into a *progressive progression.*"

"What's that?"

"Just a fancy statistical term. It simply means we're going to take a smaller percentage of that 225 the first year and a larger percentage the last year. Your percentages add up to one hundred percent, or your total goal. Here, let me show you."

After doing some quick figuring on a pocket calculator, he took the tablet and wrote down some numbers.

Steve stared at the figures Brother Keller had written. "I don't get it, Elder. Why not just divide it into equal steps. Why all the percentage stuff?"

"Why? Because you're small now. You can't do as much as you'll be able to do later on. Let me give you a simple example. When I was five years old, I could only

Figure 1
Growth Goal

	Percentage		*Amount of Average Growth*
x	12%	=	27 (first year's increase)
x	16%	=	36 (second year's increase)
225 — x	20%	=	45 (third year's increase)
x	24%	=	54 (fourth year's increase)
x	28%	=	63 (fifth year's increase)
	100%		225

take a small step. My legs were short little things. But each year as I got older, I was able to take a larger step than I could the year before. The reason is obvious. I was bigger than I was the year before.

"Steve, a large church is able to do more than a small church. It has more people, skills, and money to use. As your church increases in size, you will find yourself able to grow faster and reach more than before. So, each year you'll reach for a larger chunk of your goal. The first year will only be twelve percent of the goal. However, the second will be sixteen percent, the third twenty percent, and so on until you reach your goal. This way your goal is distributed more realistically over the five years. Let me show you your actual goals for Sunday school."

Steve studied the figures carefully. "So, by adding 27, or twelve percent of 225, to my current average, I will end up with a Sunday school goal of 102 this next year?"

"Exactly."

"Then my Sunday school goal for the second year would be 138, and the third year 183, and so on?"

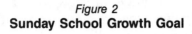

Figure 2
Sunday School Growth Goal

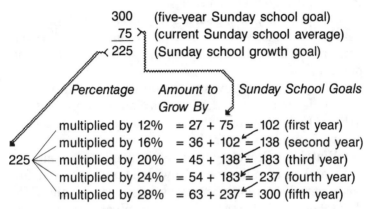

300	(five-year Sunday school goal)
75	(current Sunday school average)
225	(Sunday school growth goal)

Percentage	Amount to Grow By	Sunday School Goals
multiplied by 12%	= 27 + 75	= 102 (first year)
multiplied by 16%	= 36 + 102	= 138 (second year)
multiplied by 20%	= 45 + 138	= 183 (third year)
multiplied by 24%	= 54 + 183	= 237 (fourth year)
multiplied by 28%	= 63 + 237	= 300 (fifth year)

225

"Now you got it. Does that seem realistic to you?"

"Realistic nothing, it's too easy! I'm positive I can have my Sunday school average at 102 by the end of next year. That won't be hard!"

The old pastor sat back with a smile. "And you will have no more trouble reaching your goal the second or third year than you will the first. In fact, each year it becomes easier. You see, although the progressive progression *increases* each year, from twelve to sixteen to twenty percent and so on, your percentage of growth over the previous year *decreases*. You start out growing thirty-six percent (going from 75 to 102). The second year's growth is about thirty-five percent. The growth rate then goes down to around thirty-three percent, and your last year's growth will only be twenty-seven percent."

Steve's face lit up. "So what you're saying is that, although I'm taking a larger piece or chunk of my goal each year, my percentage of growth over the previous year is actually declining. In other words, it gets easier to reach my goal each year!"

"Yep! So if you are sure that you can reach the first year's goal, then you can be equally sure you will reach your last year's goal. Each year should be easier than the previous."

The young man's eyes got a faraway look. "Just think. In five years I'll have the largest church in my section. Why, if I can grow to 300 in five years, there's no telling where I could be in ten!"

Watching Steve's grin stretch from ear to ear, the old man had to smile too. "Now, hold on; we're not finished yet. That's only Sunday school growth, and Sunday school growth can be deceiving. What you are interested in is adult growth also. You can crank up your ol' bus and in no time reach 102 in Sunday school, yet you wouldn't have truly grown. In fact, you could bus in the whole city, but unless souls are saved, all you're doing is baby-sitting and running a social club.

"We're not looking for numbers just for numbers' sake, we're saving souls. That means children and adults *both*. Adults are what pay the bills, repair the church, teach the Sunday school classes, and build new buildings. Therefore, we need to do the same thing with adults as we have done with total attendance."

"How do we do that?"

"The same way. Tell me, of the seventy-five average attendance you now have, how many are adults? Let's say, sixteen and older."

"Sixteen and older? Let me see . . ." The young man took a minute to do some quick counting. "Almost fifty

72

I think. I can count forty-eight off hand, and I might have forgotten a few."

The old pastor used the calculator again. "That means about sixty-four percent of your attendance is adults. That's high. Your church can handle a larger Sunday school than that. With fifty adults, your Sunday school should be running around one hundred."

"I know, Elder. When the bus ministry went down the tube three years ago, we continued to grow some in adults, but we've really let our Sunday school slip."

"My recommendation, Steve, is to aim for an adult goal that is one half your total attendance goal. That would be 150. Let's take that 150, plug it into the same kind of a five-year progression that we did for Sunday school, and see what comes up."

Figure 3
Adult Growth Goal

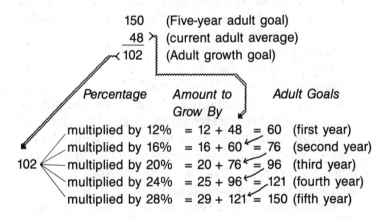

	150	(Five-year adult goal)
	48	(current adult average)
	102	(Adult growth goal)

	Percentage	Amount to Grow By		Adult Goals
	multiplied by 12%	= 12 + 48	= 60	(first year)
	multiplied by 16%	= 16 + 60	= 76	(second year)
102	multiplied by 20%	= 20 + 76	= 96	(third year)
	multiplied by 24%	= 25 + 96	= 121	(fourth year)
	multiplied by 28%	= 29 + 121	= 150	(fifth year)

The young man scratched his head, his face thoughtful, as he picked up the note pad to study the figures more closely. "Now let me be sure I understand this right. What this is showing me is that I only need twelve more adults added to the forty-eight I already have to reach my adult goal the first year?"

"Yep."

The young man's fist came down on the coffee table with a bang, fortunately not hard enough to break the glass, although the checker pieces jumped a full inch in the air. "Brother Keller," he cried, "I'm going to do it! My mind is made up. I know I can see twelve adults filled with the Holy Ghost this next year. Why, we had more than that receive the Holy Ghost last year. Boy, this is great!"

He glanced up at the old pastor. "What's wrong?"

A Christian Hobo

Brother Keller was shaking his head. "Steve, I feel sure you can reach your goal, too. But you must consider one other thing first."

"What's that?"

"Your retention factor."

"Retention factor? What's that?"

The old pastor leaned back in his chair and put his finger tips together, stretching them slowly in and out like a spider doing pushups on a mirror. "Well," he explained, "not everyone who receives the Holy Ghost stays. Wouldn't it be great if they did? Unfortunately it doesn't work that way. Jesus himself expressed this reality with the Parable of the Sower. When the sower sowed the seed, it fell on four types of ground. With the first type—the

74

hard ground—the seed never grew. In fact, it never even germinated. The birds plucked it up.

"But notice: the other three types sprouted. New life sprang up—or you could say that they received the Holy Ghost. But not all the new sprouts survived. One third was choked by the thorns, while another third was burnt by the sun. However, the last third grew into strong plants capable of bearing fruit. That's what I mean by a retention factor: the number of new plants needed to have a productive harvest.

"In the example that Jesus gave, he showed a retention factor of thirty-three percent, because one out of the three that sprouted survived. Now, I personally feel that if you don't retain at least one-third of your new converts, something's wrong. Take it for what it's worth, but I think that if you are keeping less than one out of three, you have an abnormal infant mortality rate."

Steve chewed thoughtfully on the end of the pencil as he considered this. Such an idea had never occurred to him before. "How would I figure the retention rate for my church, Elder? I have no idea what it is."

"Do you keep records of all who have been baptized and have received the Holy Ghost?"

"I . . . I used to. I started out giving baptismal certificates, but lately it's been somewhat hit and miss—meaning more miss than hit."

"Well, then, unless your memory is exceptional, you would have a difficult time figuring your retention rate. Normally, you would divide the total number that received the Holy Ghost each year into the number you retained. For example, if twenty-nine received the Holy Ghost last year, and at the end of the year you had kept seventeen, your retention rate would be 58.6% (17 divided by 29 equals .586, or 58.6%). So you kept a little over half."

"But what does that have to do with my Sunday school and adult goals?"

"Simply this," Brother Keller explained patiently. "You must have more than twelve adults receive the Holy Ghost this year if you want to end with twelve new members. How much more depends upon your past retention rate."

"So . . . what do I do now?"

"Start a new convert care system."

The young man leaned back with a sigh. He picked up the tablet again and flipped to a new page. Licking his pencil, he grinned. "All right, Elder, shoot. What's a new convert care system?"

"It's a program that raises your convert retention to as high as sixty percent. When you care for converts better, they stay better. I'm not going to explain it now, so put your pencil down. But if you promise to start a care program and keep it going, we can go on with our goal setting."

The young man threw his hands in the air. "Anything! Anything!" he almost screamed. "You name it. I'll stand on my head. I'll even eat liver and pickled pigs' feet. Whatever you say I'll do, if it will help me grow to three hundred!"

"All right," Brother Keller injected, waving his hand, "calm down and I'll show you. You're going to wake up the dead. See, you woke up Lazarus." The old dog opened one lazy eye to stare sleepily at the cause of the commotion. With a yawn he went back to sleep.

The old pastor continued. "Since you plan to start a

new convert care system, I think we can safely set your retention rate at fifty percent. That means that of all who receive the Holy Ghost you should keep at least half as solid members."

"I get it." Steve said excitedly, a little quieter this time. "So if I want twelve solid new members this year, I'll need at least twenty-four people to receive the Holy Ghost."

"Exactly—and thirty-two the second year, forty the third year, and so on. What this does is put your focus in the proper place—upon folks being saved. If you see twenty-four people receive the Holy Ghost, you will keep twelve, maybe more. With twelve new adults, your Sunday school will grow to 102 as a natural result, not just by some cute contest. Now you have your numerical goals for next year: 102 in Sunday school, twelve new adult members, and twenty-four adults to be filled with the Holy Ghost." (See figure 4.)

The young man stared at the goals on the tablet before him. "Elder," his voice now dropping down to a whisper, "you don't know how this makes me feel." His head was slowly shaking back and forth almost as if he could not believe it. "A week ago, I was ready to quit, I was so discouraged . . . I mean disappointed. All I could see were problems and headaches. With nothing to focus upon or to dream about, I drifted—you know, like a bum. That's all I was," he said with a grin, "a hobo Christian, catching the next train to nowhere. Know what my problem was, Elder? Someone gave me the ball and told me to run, yet I had no idea where to find the goal line."

The old pastor sat nodding his head. His heart was thankful that his student had caught the vision. Few principles would be as important as the lesson his pupil had learned tonight. When the young man finished talking, he spoke.

"I saw a headline in the newspaper some years ago that told of three hundred whales which had suddenly died. The whales had pursued a school of sardines and found themselves trapped in a small bay as the tide went out. The writer made a comment I'll never forget. He said, 'The tiny fish lured the giants of the sea to their death. The whales came to their demise by chasing small ends, by prostituting vast powers for insignificant goals.'[2] Steve, the church has at its disposal such vast power and potential, but often we limit God by setting our sights ridiculously low."

The young man rose to his feet for the second time that evening and walked to the broad picture window, looking out into the nighttime sky. An upper wind had swept the clouds from the heavens, and now a whole starry host sparkled like silver glitter in onyx stone. He felt almost light on his feet, a tremendous burden having been lifted from his mental shoulders.

"With God's help, Elder, I'm going to do it. I'm going to reach that three hundred, and don't be surprised if I do it in less than five years."

"That's great, son, but the next move is yours."

"How do you mean?"

"Checkers. It's your move. You're not going to get away from me that easy."

The young man threw back his head and let out a warm peal of laughter. It was his move—in more ways than one.

Figure 4
Five-Year Numerical Goals
Worksheet

Goals For Sunday School:

Five-Year Sunday School Goal *300*
Current Sunday School Average . . . . *-75*
Five-Year Growth Goal for Sunday School $\boxed{225}$

	Sunday School Growth Goals			Yearly Sunday School Goals	
x	12% = *27*	+ *75*	= *102*	Year 1 Goal
x	16% = *36*	+ *102*	= *138*	Year 2 Goal
x	20% = *45*	+ *138*	= *183*	Year 3 Goal
x	24% = *54*	+ *183*	= *237*	Year 4 Goal
x	28% = *63*	+ *237*	= *300*	Year 5 Goal

$\boxed{225}$

Goals for Adults:

Five-Year Adult Goal *150*
Current Adult Average . . . . *-48*
Five Year Growth Goal for Adults . . . . $\boxed{102}$

	Adult Growth Goals			Yearly Adult Goals	
x	12% = *12*	+ *48*	= *60*	Year 1 Goal
x	16% = *16*	+ *60*	= *76*	Year 2 Goal
x	20% = *20*	+ *76*	= *96*	Year 3 Goal
x	24% = *25*	+ *96*	= *121*	Year 4 Goal
x	28% = *29*	+ *121*	= *150*	Year 5 Goal

$\boxed{102}$

Let My People Grow

Goals for people to receive the Holy Ghost–figuring a 50% retention rate.

Year 1 Adult *Growth Goal* 12   x   2   =   24
Year 2 Adult *Growth Goal* 16   x   2   =   32
Year 3 Adult *Growth Goal* 20   x   2   =   40
Year 4 Adult *Growth Goal* 25   x   2   =   50
Year 5 Adult *Growth Goal* 29   x   2   =   58

Chapter Four

Organizing for Action

The smell of coffee, robust and fragrant, greeted Steve pleasantly as he awoke the next morning. The scent mingled deliciously with that of fried bacon and oven-baked biscuits. Staring up at the high vaultlike ceiling, he felt a moment of dreamy confusion until he remembered where he was. It was his first night in Elder Jeremiah Keller's vast, stately home.

He lay half asleep, enjoying the cozy warmth of the antique, four-postered bed. Outside he could hear the shrill cry of a mockingbird in the oak tree above his window. From the direction of the road a tractor, whining like a worn-out can opener as it shifted through its lower gears, made its way past the house toward the fields beyond. He had no idea of the time, but something told him it was growing late.

A sudden rattle of pans against dishes pulled him fully awake, alerting him that Elder Keller was moving about in the kitchen below. Steve glanced unhappily at the clock on the nightstand—9:00 A.M. "I slept too late," he muttered as he wiped the sleep from his eyes. Little wonder

81

though, for Brother Keller had kept him up past midnight talking and playing one discouraging game of checkers after another (he had lost every time). Hopping out of bed, he quickly showered and shaved, taking the time afterward to polish his shoes carefully and dress in a casual tweed sport coat and slacks. Hurrying from the bedroom, he met the elderly pastor at the foot of the stairs.

"Good morning, my friend," Elder Keller called cheerfully, one hand covered with an oversized oven mitten and the other holding a steaming mug of coffee. "I was just starting to call you. Hope you like biscuits and eggs. It's been a while since I cooked breakfast for anybody besides myself. Did you sleep well?"

"Yes, sir, I slept just fine," Steve replied, trying unsuccessfully to smother a yawn. "Your alarm clock woke me with no trouble."

Elder Keller looked puzzled. "Alarm clock? I don't use one. What do you mean?"

"Coffee and bacon. Most pleasant alarm clock I've ever smelled."

"Ah," the old man exclaimed with a toothy grin. "Come on, then, before your alarm clock gets cold. If you think it smells good, wait until you taste it. I'm as tickled as a tomcat the way my biscuits turned out."

Steve, needing no more encouragement, cheerfully followed the aged cook into the kitchen.

After breakfast Steve sat contentedly, drinking his third cup of coffee. "What's on the agenda today, Elder?" he asked.

"Well, I thought first we'd go to the church for a while. You've never been there have you? I didn't think so. I wanted to introduce you to Tommy and have him show you around. We also have several projects and ministries going that I'm sure you'd like to see."

"Will your son be at the church today?"

"Of course. He's there every day. He always arrives by eight o'clock each morning to meet with the church staff for prayer and devotions from eight to nine."

"He does that every day?"

"Well, let me back up. Every day except Monday, which is normally his day off."

"How large a staff does he have?"

Brother Keller chewed thoughtfully on a toothpick as he paused to consider. "If I remember right, twelve people are currently on the payroll. Let's see—seven teachers in the Christian school, plus Brother Thomas, who's the school principal. Then Tommy has a full-time secretary who handles the front office. Brother John McDonald is Tommy's assistant right now—a fine young man who recently graduated from Bible college. He works with the youth director some and oversees all outreach. Then there's also a bookkeeper who works part-time . . . oh yes, and Brother Tullison is our custodian and maintenance director. He's retired and lives next door to the church. He works part-time also. That makes twelve, doesn't it?"

Steve nodded in agreement. "Boy, what I could do with a staff like that. To be truthful, any kind of help would be great. You know, Elder, I've been seriously thinking about hiring a young man to work with me. It would be nice to have an assistant to help keep everything going."

The old man let out a snort. "You don't need a paid assistant."

"Why not?"

"To do what—help you preach? Not hardly. I have nothing against assistants, son—I had one for years—but before you hire an assistant you need a good secretary. That should come first. Someone who can answer phones, type letters, keep records, make phone calls, and do the hundred other things that are taking much of your time. A church is a business, the Lord's business. If you're going to reach your city, you need to open for business. A good secretary, properly trained, will not only open the church for business but also make your time more effective. That will allow you to spend more time being a pastor and soul winner. However, right now you don't need to be hiring anybody," he concluded bluntly.

Steve grinned sheepishly. "Yes, sir, I expect you're right. I'm not yet full time myself. I guess that should come first."

"There's no guess to it. Use volunteer help until the church is large enough to merit a full- or part-time position. But as long as you must work, your time and labor remain extremely divided."

The old man then stood with a groan and stretched. "My, these old bones of mine don't work too well first thing of a morning." He slapped Steve on the back. "If you'll help me clean the kitchen, we'll head for the church." Steve pushed his chair back to comply.

Keys to Growth

A half hour later they pulled into the church parking lot. Steve had glimpsed the towering church sign halfway down the street. Now he looked upon a large, beautifully designed church with neatly trimmed lawns and flower beds. An attractive broad-board fence surrounded the entire ten acres, enclosing not only the church but also the small caretaker's cottage that sat off to the left. A long line of white and red buses, eight in all, stood smartly like soldiers in dress formation, angling down one side of the property. A paved parking lot extended down each side and across the back.

The front of the sanctuary reminded Steve of the bow of a ship—tall and tapered together in a sharp point. It was faced with ornamental stone, which was also used for the long planters in the front. About halfway up the rock face, a large, clear, stained-glass window revealed a crystal chandelier that hung, he guessed, above the vestibule. A white steeple crowned the rock face. Two large wings, looking like small-scale replicas of the main building, extended out either side in the back. One wing, Brother Keller explained, was for education, and the other was a social hall.

They parked in the special "Reserved For Pastor" spot—Tommy Keller's car was gone—and Elder Keller led the way through the glass front doors and to the long, marble-colored counter that divided the secretary's office from the main foyer. The secretary, a pleasant woman in her fifties and precisely Pentecostal from head to foot, glanced up and smiled warmly as they entered.

"Sister Jo Ann, I want you to meet Brother Steve Martin, pastor from Springville. He's staying with me for a few days, and I'll be showing him around. He may even want to talk to you about some of the office procedures. That's up to him. Later, I'll want you to photocopy for him some of the departmental material we have.

"Jo Ann is our girl Friday, Steve. She's the real one

who keeps things going when Tommy's out of town. I don't think we could survive around here without her. She used to be my secretary before I retired. She and her husband, Rex, came to the Lord here about sixteen years ago."

Brother Keller turned back to Jo Ann. "Is my son here? His car wasn't out front."

"No, sir. He went to see the architect about the new blueprints. He said he'd be back around noon."

"All right, we'll wait back in his office."

They walked through large double doors and into the spacious sanctuary. The interior took Steve by surprise. He was not sure what he had expected, but definitely not what he saw. It was the first sanctuary he had ever seen done in pink—well, perhaps not pink; more of a light, dusty rose—and offset with lilac and burgundy. Shiny chrome was splashed in various places throughout the sanctuary in the planters, the light fixtures, and oddly, the pulpit, which was custom designed from plexiglass and chrome. The back wall behind the pulpit sported glass building block, upon which hung a beautiful, stained-glass, dove-and-flame decoration. The overall effect was somewhat modern, yet extremely attractive.

The sanctuary colors, Brother Keller explained as they walked up the center aisle, had been designed by a church member who worked professionally in interior design. They had wanted something that would be attractive yet different, and that would not be out of style in a few years.

It was definitely that.

Mounting the steps, they turned to the left and entered a door off the platform, which led into the pastor's study.

The ample room was comfortably furnished and brightly lit. Two walls displayed an impressive collection of pastoral books and commentaries. A magnificent seascape hung directly behind the broad oak desk to their right. On the walls, shelves, and desk were other artifacts and mementos of nautical design, some hanging and others displayed on individual stands. In the far corner a world globe stood on a pedestal alongside an enormous handmade model ship, a double-masted schooner, obviously made by the same craftsman as the one in Elder Keller's living room.

However, what caught Steve's eye as he walked into the room was something facing them on the wall as they entered. Within a tall, oak-and-glass frame hung a professionally drawn organizational chart. Names, boxes, and lines depicted various departments and ministries, all blending together into beautiful, symmetrical balance. Steve walked over to examine it as Elder Keller hung up their coats. (See figure 5.)

"Looks like quite an organization," Steve said, his voice betraying his admiration. "Are all these department heads full time?"

"No," Elder Keller replied, "only the school principal. The rest are simply faithful saints in the church."

Steve examined each name and department, closely reading the various ministries and responsibilities of each. "I thought you said the assistant pastor—McDonald, wasn't it—directed all outreach. His name isn't on any department."

The retired pastor eased himself down in the upholstered chair behind the desk. "That's right. But, remember, I said he oversees the various outreach

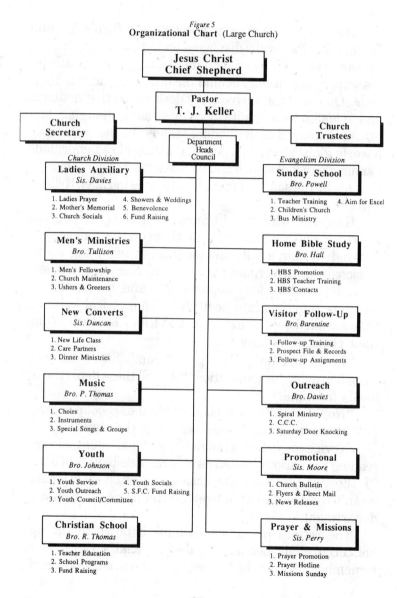

Figure 5
Organizational Chart (Large Church)

Jesus Christ
Chief Shepherd

Pastor
T. J. Keller

Church Secretary

Church Trustees

Department Heads Council

Church Division

Ladies Auxiliary
Sis. Davies

1. Ladies Prayer   4. Showers & Weddings
2. Mother's Memorial   5. Benevolence
3. Church Socials   6. Fund Raising

Men's Ministries
Bro. Tullison

1. Men's Fellowship
2. Church Maintenance
3. Ushers & Greeters

New Converts
Sis. Duncan

1. New Life Class
2. Care Partners
3. Dinner Ministries

Music
Bro. P. Thomas

1. Choirs
2. Instruments
3. Special Songs & Groups

Youth
Bro. Johnson

1. Youth Service   4. Youth Socials
2. Youth Outreach   5. S.F.C. Fund Raising
3. Youth Council/Committee

Christian School
Bro. R. Thomas

1. Teacher Education
2. School Programs
3. Fund Raising

Evangelism Division

Sunday School
Bro. Powell

1. Teacher Training   4. Aim for Excel
2. Children's Church
3. Bus Ministry

Home Bible Study
Bro. Hall

1. HBS Promotion
2. HBS Teacher Training
3. HBS Contacts

Visitor Follow-Up
Bro. Barentine

1. Follow-up Training
2. Prospect File & Records
3. Follow-up Assignments

Outreach
Bro. Davies

1. Spiral Ministry
2. C.C.C.
3. Saturday Door Knocking

Promotional
Sis. Moore

1. Church Bulletin
2. Flyers & Direct Mail
3. News Releases

Prayer & Missions
Sis. Perry

1. Prayer Promotion
2. Prayer Hotline
3. Missions Sunday

88

ministries, meaning he helps the directors and motivates the workers. But he isn't the director over any one department. Brother McDonald displays tremendous potential, so he'll probably move on in a year or two to evangelize or pastor. We need department heads whom we can count on being here for the long haul. We used to put our assistant pastor in charge of all outreach, or all youth ministries, and every time the assistant left, the department would fall apart. That's not good."

The young man glanced over his shoulder and nodded his head in agreement. He then turned his attention back to the chart, tracing the glass with his finger, carefully studying departments on the right-hand side. "What did you do, Elder, to build a church like this? What outreaches did you have? What methods or programs did you use?"

Elder Keller leaned back in the chair and crossed his legs. "Probably the same ones you have used: home Bible study, bus ministry, door knocking, Sunday school, revivals, and so on."

The young man turned back around with a puzzled look. "But why have they worked for you and not for me?"

The elderly pastor grinned mischievously. "Steve, come sit down. You have your notebook? Good. I want to reveal to you the secret of developing a successful, growing church. Few men have discovered this truth. Are you ready? All right. Write the following word: w - o - r- k. Now circle it, underline it, put an exclamation mark . . ."

"Come on!" Steve exclaimed. "I'm serious! I know it takes work. Yet if work was the answer I'd be averaging a thousand. How come my bus ministry flopped and yours didn't? Why do your people teach home Bible studies and mine won't? You must be doing something new or different.''

The old man sat chuckling. "Son, I wish I could tell you in three easy steps, but it's not that simple. You're asking about outreaches and programs, and frankly, I don't know of any new outreaches and programs—only new variations of the same old ones. Like breakfast cereals, they slap on 'new and improved,' give it a new name, and send it out again. Truthfully, I can't improve upon the three key principles of growth I heard fifty years ago.''

"Which are?''

"The first is simple, yet it can't be overlooked. It's having an undying personal devotion and walk with God. Many a pastor down through the years—I could name you a dozen right now—has stumbled because in his zeal to build a large church he neglected his own spiritual health. Hear me well, young man, if you are too busy to pray and study, you're just flat too busy. A carnal pastor will have a carnal church, and a carnal church doesn't grow—it enrolls, country-club style.

"The second key principle is as important as the first. A pastor must have a sensitivity and responsiveness to the Holy Ghost—in preaching, counseling, and dealing with people. I've seen it happen time and again, son. When a man doesn't follow the Spirit's direction—meaning he can't tell if the Lord is speaking or not—he'll invariably follow his flesh. As a result, he'll always be doing something foolish. The final outcome will be that he will continually lose people because they lose faith and confidence in him. This is why fasting and prayer are vitally important. They increase your spiritual perception.

"The last key is less dramatic than the first two, but no less important. It's knowing how to organize, delegate, and manage the work of God in a way that brings results—and by results I mean growth. A careless steward will never direct a large household. Nor will an incompetent farmer ever manage a large vineyard. A pastor is no different. He's an administrator whether he likes it or not, and how well he manages his church determines, to a great extent, how large his church can grow."

Steve still looked puzzled. "I know what delegation is, but I thought organization and management meant the same thing."

Elder Keller shook his head. "No, they're quite different, although they must go hand in hand. Organization is best defined as 'arranging an administrative structure for unified planning and effort.' The key word here is *structure*. Your organizational structure, whether it looks like that one on the wall or not, tells you who does what and when. It defines authority, responsibilities, positions, interdepartmental relationships, and the like. In other words, when the whole place blows up, people know what to do; and when the dust settles, someone is still in charge."

"And management?"

"Where organization is a thing like that wall chart over there, management is an action. Management is what you do to make your structure work. It's directing, motivating, supervising, and leading the people within your organizational structure."

Outside, the Christian school had let out for recess. The happy squeals of the children could be plainly heard through the window as they began running and playing with energetic zeal.

Organizing for Action

The young man again stared at the multicolored chart. Several seconds elapsed before he spoke. "You know, Elder, this depicts one of my greatest problems. I like to think I have a sufficient grasp of the first two key principles you mentioned—although I'm sure I have room for improvement—but if I could only develop an organization like this," his hand swept across the glass, "I'm sure my church could get somewhere."

Steve glanced back at the older pastor and grinned ruefully. "I sometimes feel as if I'm using that new educational puzzle that's just come out. I understand it's supposed to prepare kids for today's complex world—no matter how you put it together, it doesn't come out right."

The old man laughed agreeably. "I know what you mean. At one time everything I tried to organize fell apart too. I finally threw up my hands and said, 'Forget it. I'll just preach and pray, and leave the rest to God.' However I soon found that I would grow to a certain point— somewhere around seventy—and just stop. I couldn't climb over that hump."

"Because of no organization?"

Elder Keller nodded. "You see, Steve, a church will usually grow from zero to around seventy primarily from the pastor's efforts. He will be the main driving force behind everything. He will also be the primary soul winner. Up to that point little organization is needed. He might have several departments—Sunday School, New Convert Care, Ladies Auxiliary, Outreach, and maybe

Men's Fellowship (which could also oversee church maintenance duties) or Youth Ministry—but not much more. In fact, too large an organization might hinder his growth. That's because a pastor whose church is averaging below seventy needs to focus on just two areas: much personal evangelism by himself and his people—home Bible studies, door knocking, bringing visitors, witnessing—and powerful, evangelistic services. He should find a good outreach method or tool that he has confidence in, then use it for all it's worth. With this kind of focus, along with ample prayer and determination, a church can grow to a Sunday morning average of around sixty or seventy.

"However, after the church reaches about seventy, something happens. He finds himself having to spend a large block of his time being a pastor instead of a soul winner. The church is large enough now to demand almost his full attention, leaving him less time to visit, knock doors, and teach Bible studies. But hear me well, young man. If you ever stop being a soul winner, even after your church gets large, your growth will greatly decrease. People learn better by example than by command. But for now, if you wish to continue growing, you must organize, and organizing means multiplying your ministry through other people."

"So I need to set myself up with twelve departments like you have."

"Not at all. You may not need that many at this point. Keep your organization simple, Steve. Where most pastors get into trouble is trying to organize too much too quickly. You most likely only need some basic departments."

93

"Like what?"

The old pastor rose from the desk chair and came over to stand next to Steve beside the wall chart. "Well, every church is different. I can only speak for myself and what I did. Remember I told you the church has two primary objectives; to win the lost and to perfect the saints? Those two objectives should dictate your structure. Now, look at the chart." Elder Keller pointed to it with one long, skinny finger.

"You will see these same two areas. The departments on the left side—the Church Division—are inward directed to help the church. The departments on the right side— the Evangelism Division—are outward directed to reach the world. Of course, some departments do both. Even the church ministries have some outreach activities. Ladies Auxiliary and Men's Fellowship both get involved in soul winning, yet it's not their primary function. Or take the Music Department for example. We use music as an outreach quite often, but its main purpose is to promote an atmosphere of worship. Some evangelism departments also minister to the church, yet again, their main function is to win souls."

The old man put his hand on Steve's shoulder. "Let me show you how I first set up my church." They both walked to the desk and sat down. Brother Keller took out a piece of paper.

"When I first organized this church we averaged around forty. I had already organized a Sunday school, and my wife oversaw Ladies Auxiliary and New Convert Care. We also had a youth leader, and one of my men helped me push outreach and home Bible study. We had just developed a small choir when I decided to establish a more organized departmental structure." (See figure 6.)

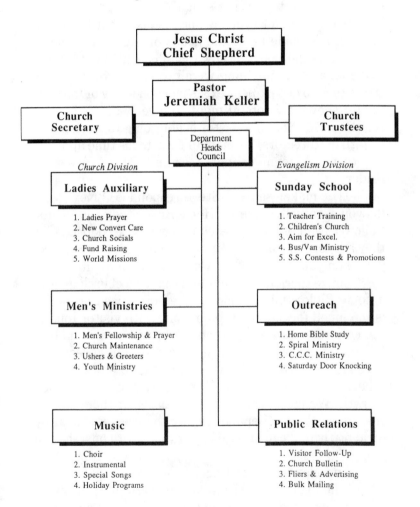

Figure 6
Organizational Chart (Small Church)

**Jesus Christ
Chief Shepherd**

**Pastor
Jeremiah Keller**

**Church
Secretary**

Department
Heads
Council

**Church
Trustees**

Church Division

Ladies Auxiliary

1. Ladies Prayer
2. New Convert Care
3. Church Socials
4. Fund Raising
5. World Missions

Evangelism Division

Sunday School

1. Teacher Training
2. Children's Church
3. Aim for Excel.
4. Bus/Van Ministry
5. S.S. Contests & Promotions

Men's Ministries

1. Men's Fellowship & Prayer
2. Church Maintenance
3. Ushers & Greeters
4. Youth Ministry

Outreach

1. Home Bible Study
2. Spiral Ministry
3. C.C.C. Ministry
4. Saturday Door Knocking

Music

1. Choir
2. Instrumental
3. Special Songs
4. Holiday Programs

Public Relations

1. Visitor Follow-Up
2. Church Bulletin
3. Fliers & Advertising
4. Bulk Mailing

95

The young man studied the paper for a moment. "Why do both of your charts have 'Department Heads Council' at the top? What's that?"

"A department heads council is just what the name implies. It's made up of the heads of each department. I put this on the chart to show that all department leaders make up a team, meaning we all work together, and to stress that no department exists independently of the rest. It also shows my commitment to meet with them on a regular basis. Son, if a pastor is not going to work closely with his directors, he shouldn't waste his time appointing them. A team cannot operate with an absentee leader."

"That makes sense," Steve responded. "Now, why did you eventually separate Home Bible Study and Visitor Follow-Up out of the Outreach Department? I noticed that they are separate departments on your current structure, yet when you started, they were both under Outreach."

"Past experience. I've found that as a church grows, a home Bible study ministry, when organized properly, is too much for one man to do along with visitor follow-up. One man with one responsibility will always do better than one man divided in two different directions, because the latter will always emphasize one over the other. But the truth is, both ministries are critical for growth. We can't afford to have either of them suffer, so I made them a department by themselves. Also, by dividing them, I can keep in better touch with how they're doing."

"And New Convert Care?"

"When you see my new convert care program, son, you'll understand. It works extremely well, but when you have a steady flow of new converts, it requires someone's complete attention."

The young man nodded. "But if dividing the responsibilities into departments makes them function better, why not do that with everything? You know, make each individual ministry its own department and put them all on the council."

Elder Keller shook his head emphatically. "Won't work. Many pastors have tried doing exactly that, but they can't effectively supervise that many people. In the business world it's called *span of control*. When you get more than twelve or fourteen departments you can't manage them properly. The Lord chose twelve as the number of government, and the business world has discovered this to be the best number also. With more than twelve you have three problems: lack of supervision, difficulty reaching any group agreement, and meetings and departmental planning sessions taking too long. Start with around six or eight departments and slowly add as needed. But never allow over fourteen departments. Twelve's best."

"So how do I know what should be made a department? And what about smaller ministries, such as children's church and tape ministry? Do they just float around without supervision?"

"Oh no. Although smaller, they are still important. Really, in the Lord's church there is no ministry that is more important than another. Paul told us that every part of the body is critical. The criterion for determining what needs to be a department is whether a ministry's activities need to be coordinated with the other departments. Then, too, some ministries need more supervision to function than others.

"For example, the activities of the outreach ministry must be woven together with all the other departmental activities. Also, an outreach ministry tends to fall apart if you don't stay right on top of it to ensure its success. That is not true of, let's say, the tape ministry or the ushers. They tend to do fine with only minimum supervision. You should place these kinds of ministries within your chosen departments.

"This is important," he continued, "because a prime reason for your departmental council is so that you can touch any area, position, or responsibility in your church. This makes your time more effective. The activities of your young married's fellowship may not be critical enough to merit a position on the council, so it may come under the Youth Department umbrella. The same may apply to youth clubs, children's church, and so on. Don't take me wrong, it's not that they are any less important, it's a matter of setting priorities. You must draw the line somewhere."

Steve's brow creased slightly as he listened to Brother Keller. "I think I follow you, sir. What you're saying is that every job or position in the church should appear on the organizational flow chart somewhere, either as a major department, or as a ministry within your major departments."

"Yep. You'll find that works best."

A Blessing or a Curse

The young man paused, then shook his head. "That sounds fine, Elder, but although it looks convincing on paper, it doesn't always work. You see, I've done all this before. I've drawn up charts on paper. Maybe not exactly like this, yet the same idea. Just putting a name in a box doesn't get the job done. Like my bus ministry—it completely flopped."

Elder Keller leaned back with a sigh. "As I said, Steve, the hard part is not organizing the ministry, it's managing it. There's a difference."

The young man frowned again. "I don't follow you. I know how to manage as well as the next guy."

"Do you? Are you sure? Management is not a natural talent. It's a skill that is learned, and it's more difficult than it looks.

"For example, I took my boys water skiing once, and a friend of theirs wanted to go too. I asked him, 'You know how to ski, son?' 'Sure!' he said, so I let him come. The first time he tried to get up, arms, legs, and skis went everywhere. The second time around—same results. After the third try I asked him again, 'You know how to ski, son?' 'Oh yes,' he replied. So I tried another question, 'Son, have you ever skied before?' 'No,' he said, 'but it looks easy.'

"The same problem exists with management. It looks easy—just smile, say a few kind words, write a letter, lead some meetings—easy. It's not that easy!"

"At the risk of sounding ignorant, Elder, what exactly do you mean by management?"

"Well, management can be broken into three parts. The first is leadership, which means to inspire and motivate to action. The second is administration, which involves delegation and training. The third is supervision, which includes accountability and control. However, a more candid definition of management is simply 'the art of getting things done through other people.'"

The young man slowly nodded his head. "So you're saying that the reason my bus ministry failed is because, although the route went well when I did it, when I pulled out, I improperly delegated the responsibility to someone else?"

"It sounds that way, and the problem is extremely common. I have a friend who pastors a small church in a neighboring state. He's pastored there for years, preaching to a tiny handful of people. He personally does every little task in the church, most of which could easily be delegated to others. I asked him one day, 'Walt, what in the world are you doing?' He replied, 'I do everything myself. I mow the lawn, I clean the church, I run off bulletins, I wash windows, I do it all. That way I know it is done properly.' And that revealed exactly why he never grew. If you want to grow, son, you must multiply your ministry through other people. Jesus did this, which is why the church spread so rapidly."

Key Concept Three

**Thou shalt have unfailing faith
in thy people, for they are laborers
together with thee in God's vineyard.**

"All right, you've convinced me, but how am I going to convince my people? I've got some who believe that management and organization are only worldly substitutes for the leading of the Spirit."

"Look, Steve, you need to teach your people that

management is nothing more than a tool. Tools can be good or bad, depending upon the hands that hold them. The question isn't whether the *tool* is spiritual or carnal, but whether *we* are spiritual or carnal. If you want to be carnal in your service for Jesus Christ, you don't have to use management to do so. Being organized doesn't mean you're carnal any more than being unorganized means you're spiritual.

"Here's a statement I want you to write down. Let it sink deeply into your heart so you will never forget it. *There are some things that God will bless as a supplement but curse as a substitute.*[1] I'm not suggesting that management and organization become substitutes for the leading of the Spirit. I am saying that this kind of tool can make our labor for God more effective.

"Biblical examples of management abound," Elder Keller continued. "Joseph's organizational abilities brought him favor, not only in Potiphar's house, but also in jail. The Lord finally led him to be second to Pharaoh over all Egypt. Moses gave a good example of delegation when, at his father-in-law's advice, he divided up the people into fifties, hundreds, and thousands and appointed supervisors. David's ability to organize and lead the armies of Israel was legendary. And his son Solomon supervised the construction of the richest temple in history. Ezra's leadership brought the Jews out of captivity and organized them to rebuild the Temple.

"Now, Nehemiah has long been viewed as a master of management. He unified the people to rebuild the walls, delegated the many responsibilities, and then supervised the work to completion. However, nothing equals the Lord's example. His training of the Twelve involved every

101

phase of management: inspiration, motivation, delegation, training, and accountability. In fact, the Lord's training resulted in the quick solution of the first great crisis in the church. Acts chapter six records the appointment of deacons to give the apostles more time to minister. That's what proper management is all about—getting things done through other people."

Steve stood up and walked over to the wall, gesturing to the organizational chart again. "But how can I do this and make it work? How do you delegate?"

"The best way is to find the right kind of bones."

"What?"

The old pastor's face split into a wide grin. "In the anatomy of a church, Steve, you'll find four kinds of bones. I've yet to see a church in which they did not exist. The first kind is Wish-bones. These people always hope that someone else will do the work. Getting them to do anything is usually more work than doing it yourself. The second kind is Jaw-bones. We have an abundance of these in this church. They are quick to talk about what needs to be done, yet that's all they do—talk. Try and suggest that they do something, and see the response you get. The third type is Knuckle-bones. They simply knock what everybody else is doing without doing anything themselves. The truth of the matter is, they will never be satisfied with what anybody does. They're incurable complainers. But thank God for the last kind, Back-bones, because they get the job done. They'll get down and work and sweat and stay at it until it's finished. What you must first do is identify this highly select group."

"By that you mean those who are best qualified?"

"No, that's not what I mean. You'll find that some

folks are highly qualified yet completely unfaithful. You can't depend on them for anything. Ability without dependability is worthless. It's like a car without a motor—looks nice, but doesn't go anywhere. Faithfulness must come first."

The young pastor shook his head in frustration. "I'm sorry to be asking so many questions, Elder, but this is all so new to me. You say I need faithful people to do the work. Fine, but how do I know whom I can trust? How do you identify faithfulness?"

"Start your potential leaders out slowly, Steve. Don't give responsibility without first knowing how the person will react. The essence of good management lies first in good delegation. If you choose the wrong person, you'll spend longer correcting the problem than it would have taken to do the job yourself. Some people just can't be depended upon to do anything—except perhaps make dandruff."

The young man's look of frustration turned into a wide smile. "Elder, you do have a way with words. However, when do talent and ability come into the picture?"

"Talent and ability, Steve, are the icing on the cake. If people have talent, great. If not, train them. You see, this is where many pastors fail in delegation. They look at their people and say, 'Since I have no one talented in that area, I'll just do it myself,' and their church never grows. Yet a one-man band can't match the quality of a hundred-piece orchestra. If pastors would take their faithful workers and train them, before long they would have faithfulness and talent both."

The young man thought about this for a moment, nodding slowly. "I understand you, Elder, and I agree in principle. Unfortunately, it doesn't always work that easily. Take my Sunday school superintendent for example. Brother Marker is extremely faithful. I couldn't ask for a more loyal and dependable man. But two weeks ago he up and quit his position. He said he doesn't have time anymore, but I know that's just an excuse. What went wrong?"

"Steve, when a faithful, dependable person accepts a position and they still don't do the job, then you know the reason for their procrastination is usually twofold. The first reason is they don't know fully *what* they are supposed to do."

"Hold it," Steve interrupted. "I told him what to do. When he first started I sat down with him for about two hours in my office one afternoon and explained his responsibilities."

"Did you put them in writing?"

"Uh . . . no."

"Does he have a photographic memory?"

"No, sir."

"Did he take careful notes?"

"Not that I remember."

"Then he doesn't know what to do. You see, Steve, a person retains less than ten percent of what he hears. If you didn't put those responsibilities in writing, then I doubt your superintendent truly knows what to do, except what he learned by trial and error. A person without a written job description will usually do as little as possible for fear of overstepping his boundaries."

The young man scratched his head thoughtfully, then his face brightened. "Well, Elder, do you mind if I photocopy your job descriptions? I'll just give Brother Marker a copy."

"Yes, son, I do mind—not your getting a copy, but your giving one to Brother Marker. A canned, precooked job description is worthless. For job descriptions to do any good, they must be custom written to fit you and your church's needs. After all, isn't that the reason for giving it—to explain what you want done?"

The young man looked sheepish. "Uh . . . yes, I guess so. I'll only use yours as a guideline to write my own."

The old pastor nodded. "That's a good way to do it. Read mine through, mark out what doesn't apply, add what's missing, then retype it. Every person, regardless of how small the position, has a right to know what you expect of him. I would hate for God to expect me to do something and have no idea what it was. Your directors are no different. Thankfully the Lord gave us a written job description. It's called the Bible."

"Hey, that's right!"

"One last thing, son. Once that job description is written, sit down with the person and go over it point by point. Make sure he not only reads it but understands it. That job description is not a document to be locked away in some filing cabinet; it's a tool. It should be used, examined, and updated every year."

The young man nodded as he wrote. "All right, sir. But you said there are two reasons why a job isn't accomplished. That's only one."

"The second reason for a person to procrastinate is that he doesn't know fully *how* to do the job. You can know what to do without knowing how to do it. Let me give you an example.

"Many years ago as a teen-ager, I took a job as the delivery manager in a furniture store. Now, I had never managed a delivery department in my life. Thankfully, when I started working, the owner showed me step by step how to operate that department. He put it in writing. I followed the pattern he gave me to the letter. After all, he knew the job; I sure didn't! But after six months I noticed something. I had changed the pattern. I had improved it. You see, once I knew the job, I saw where the operation could be made more efficient. Yet that was impossible when I first started. I needed a pattern to follow.

"Steve, ninety-five percent of the time when you ask people to take a position, they have never done that job before. They have never been an outreach director, or youth director, or Ladies Auxiliary director. If they don't have some kind of an example to follow, they will often do nothing. If you don't train them and show them how to do the job, who will? How will they learn?"

The young man shrugged his shoulders. "I thought the job description did that."

"Only if you put it there. That is why a job description needs to be detailed. You might tell your Sunday school superintendent that he is responsible to hold an attendance drive every Easter. Good; now he knows what to do. But he's never held an attendance drive before. He doesn't know how to do it. What kind of results do you think he'll have?"

"Probably lousy."

"Right. Then discouragement sets in. You must show him how. I followed three steps when I trained my directors. I first told them how (in writing), then I showed them how (they worked with me), then I let them do it (I only observed). Granted, you have to give a man room to make mistakes. However, proper training will minimize mistakes.''

The young man sat back, staring at the chart on the desk, his mind racing. ''My,'' he said slowly. ''Brother Keller, if I could get my directors trained and all doing their jobs . . . I could almost kick back, relax, and let the church run itself!''

''Fat chance,'' the old pastor said with a smile. ''Delegation is not so you can do nothing; it is so you can do the things only you can do. Those cannot be delegated. You still have all your pastoral duties: preaching, visiting the sick, counseling, and so on. All delegation does is allow you to focus on the priorities of your ministry.

''But the process of delegation will fall apart if you don't include your proper supervision. An old management proverb says, 'People don't do what you expect; they do what you inspect.' Ninety percent of delegation fails because the leader fails to make his directors accountable for their duties. Without accountability, you abandon the man and the job. You see, the proper definition of delegation is 'entrusting responsibility and authority to other people while still maintaining a management check on those responsibilities.' Even though you delegate a job, the responsibility to see that it's done still rests on your shoulders.''

''How do you suggest I do that?''

''Any number of ways—departmental council meetings, monthly reports, and tag-in sessions, to name a few.''

The young man leaned his head back and closed his eyes, trying to get it all straight in his mind. With his eyes still shut, he began to count slowly on his fingers. "First you design your organizational structure, making the key ministries individual departments. Then you write job descriptions for each position needed. Next, with much prayer, you choose faithful people for each position according to the talents they have. This is followed up with personal training, giving each person a pattern to follow. Last, you place accountability on each position to ensure that the job is carried out." His eyes flew open. "I miss anything?" he asked with a grin.

"No, sounds fine."

"And by doing all that I'll be back on the road to growth?"

"No, you won't," the old man stated flatly.

"What?" the young man cried, his mouth hanging open. "What's wrong? What did I miss?"

"You didn't miss anything. But doing those five things will not guarantee growth."

"What do you mean?"

"Just what I said. Organization and management will never bring growth by themselves anymore than a new building will bring growth by itself. Those represent things, and revival is not a thing. Revival is a moving of the Spirit, and only as we yield to the Spirit will revival come. What organization does is *prepare* you for revival. To wait until after the revival to organize is to lose most of your harvest. While you're trying to get your act together, the grain lies rotting in the field. If you desire growth, son, then prepare and plan as if it's already coming. That's putting your faith into action. That way, when the Lord sends you an abundance of fish, your nets won't break and your boat won't sink."

Steve nodded slowly. "All right, but what brings revival? What can I do that will guarantee results?"

"Son, the proper application of several basic Bible principles will do more to bring revival than . . ."

Elder Keller's explanation was interrupted by a scream that shattered the stillness of the church.

Chapter Five

Like a Mighty Army

The scream still echoed faintly in the sanctuary as Steve rushed from the pastor's office and sprinted down the center aisle of the sanctuary toward the foyer. Bursting through the double doors into the vestibule, he quickly took in the situation before him.

Then he grinned.

Sister Jo Ann, the church secretary, leaned against the far wall, her face deep red with embarrassment. She fanned herself with one hand and held onto a hall table with the other, all the while laughing and crying simultaneously. Beside her, a door stood open into what looked like a supply room. On both walls reams of paper and boxes stacked the shelves from floor to ceiling. A tall, portly, middle-aged man in a three-piece, gray, pin-stripe suit stood just inside the supply room door, a boyish grin spread from ear to ear, his eyes twinkling merrily.

"What happened? What's wrong?" Elder Keller cried as he came puffing up beside Steve, his face creased with worry and fear.

"It's nothing, Dad," the tall gentleman called, "I just

111

surprised Sister Jo Ann a bit."

"A bit!" Jo Ann shrieked. "I about died from fright!"

Seeing his father's puzzled look, Tommy Keller explained. "I picked up a box of copier paper on the way back from the architect and came in the supply room's outside entrance. I closed the outside door without thinking to turn on the light switch and—"

"And," Jo Ann interrupted, "I opened the door at the same moment to get some envelopes. I didn't know he'd come in, so when I opened the door, all I saw was this massive, shadowy figure reaching for me . . ."

She began to laugh again; this time the other three joined in.

"I was only reaching for the light switch," Tommy chuckled. "But you should've seen the look on her face. You'd have thought she saw the devil himself." He paused and looked at Steve. Still smiling, he held out his hand. "You must be Steve Martin. I'm Tommy Keller."

Tommy Keller looked to be in his mid forties. He was a large man, broad across the shoulders and thick in the chest. He stood every bit of six foot four and reminded Steve of a football linebacker he had seen. He combed his light-brown hair straight back, which unfortunately emphasized a deep, receding hairline. His eyes, like his father's, seemed to be laughing even when a smile wasn't present. Wrinkles lined the corners of his eyes and mouth, giving Steve the impression that Tommy Keller enjoyed laughing at life.

Steve reached out and shook the big man's hand. "Good to meet you, Brother Keller. Your father has spoken much of you."

"Wondered why my ears were burning," Tommy said

112

with a teasing smile. "Hope it's been good, yet the Lord knows he probably had little good to tell."

"Oh, yes, sir, it's been outstanding," Steve assured him. "He's quite proud of you and the way the church is growing."

"Don't let him kid you," Tommy returned. "I don't do anything except what he's taught me. When you take a church in as good a condition as this one, a feller couldn't help but have results."

Tommy Keller turned to his father. "I stopped by to see if you two wanted some lunch. I also need to get your opinion on several points concerning the annual departmental planning retreat next week."

Elder Keller put his hand on Steve's shoulder. "Hungry? Even if you're not, I am, and you're probably ready for a break."

"Sure am. I'm about to get writer's cramp," Steve answered, rubbing his wrist ruefully. He looked at Tommy. "I think your dad is trying to graduate me from Bible college in five easy lessons."

Tommy laughed. "If you only get five lessons, my friend, he's shortchanging you. Come on, we'll go in my car." Still talking and cracking jokes, Tommy ushered the other two out the front door.

Fifteen Families Saved

Ten minutes later they sat in a family-style steakhouse just down the street from the church. Elder Keller and Tommy sat on one side of the table and Steve on the other.

After taking their coats and hanging them up, Tommy looked across at Steve and whistled softly. "Boy, Dad told me how the Lord brought the two of you together. That's beautiful! But did Dad tell you it's not the first time something like this has happened? Maybe not in this exact way, but the Lord's been directing pastors to Dad for help one way or another for several years. In fact, some of the pastors he has helped have larger churches now than Apostolic Tabernacle."

"But few have mothered five new churches as he has either," Steve defended.

"Oh, I'm not saying that to be negative," Tommy replied. "Nobody's more proud of what Dad has done than I. I strongly believe that the mother-church concept is the only realistic plan we have of reaching into our nonevangelized areas. That's why I'm planning now to begin a cell ministry of home Bible fellowships. It's the easiest way to plant new churches. What I mean is, the principles that Dad's sharing with you really do work. Those churches that have grown have been the ones whose pastors have taken these principles to heart and used them."

Elder Keller put his hand on his son's shoulder. "I don't think you have to worry about Steve, son. He asks too many questions to be taking anything lightly. Not only is he a walking question box, but he has the most important ingredient needed for growth: a burning desire. This young man's absolutely determined to reach his city."

Steve said nothing, feeling somewhat embarrassed at the unexpected compliment.

"Now, son," Elder Keller spoke to Tommy, "what did you want to ask me?"

"It's about the departmental planning retreat next week. As far as I know, all the department heads plan to attend. But currently the bus ministry is still a ministry within the Sunday School Department. However, with bus ministry winning so many adults lately, I'm wanting to expand and encourage it more. I'm considering taking it out of the Sunday School Department and making it a separate department by itself. That way the director will sit on the department heads council, attend the annual planning retreat, hand in a monthly report, and I can work with him more closely."

The elderly preacher considered this for a moment, his brow frowning slightly. "I understand what you're doing, Tommy, and from the standpoint of helping that department grow, you are correct. Any time you turn a ministry into a department and work with it on a regular basis, that department will grow more rapidly.

"On the other hand, one more department will give you thirteen on the department heads council. This is still within your span of control. Yet, remember, when you start your home Bible fellowships, it will need to be an individual department also. With fourteen departments, you risk losing some of your effectiveness in supervision."

Tommy Keller slowly nodded, biting softly on his lower lip. "Let me pray about it, Dad. Maybe I can find another way to encourage and promote bus ministry. But, to tell the truth, I almost think it would be worth the risk. We're have a regular revival on the bus routes."

Steve had been listening to the two preachers with rapt attention. Now he asked the question that burned inside him. "Pastor Keller, what are you doing in bus ministry to win adults? I never saw any adults saved from our efforts. I thought bus ministry was simply a ministry to children."

Just then the young waitress came with their coffee and took their order. Tommy slowly stirred in sugar before he replied, choosing his words carefully. "I don't want to sound critical of what another church is doing or how it operates its buses, Steve. For many years, we ran ours exactly like everyone else, and like you, saw only limited results for the expense. However, we recently started using the Parentreach program of bus ministry. The results are tremendous."

"Parentreach?"

"Parentreach is a concept that redirects the focus of bus ministry from numbers to souls. Like many, we found ourselves caught in the numbers game. We pushed simply to fill our buses to capacity—often to a dangerous capacity. Numbers alone became our goal, and we got exactly what we sought for—numbers—and little else. We had kids running and screaming and pouring out our pews. It didn't take long before the tremendous time and expense squeezed us dry. Our bus workers became burned out, and with the huge number of children in each classroom, our teachers could not teach effectively and became discouraged. Like many other pastors, I often heard the complaint of baby-sitting.

"When I was just about ready to dump our bus ministry, the Lord directed us to change our strategy. We now limit the number of houses with which our route captains can work—eight to twelve at the most. When our route captains go on Saturday visitation, they only visit those eight to twelve homes. And it's not to see little Johnny Jones, it's to see Mr. and Mrs. Jones. The sole reason for Saturday visitation is to talk to the parents and try to get a home Bible study.

"The way it works is this. We put each set of homes—eight to twelve in a group—on a four-month schedule. For

116

the first two months, that route captain's main goal is to make a friend of those parents. The saying that you must win their friendship before you can win their souls is true. So anything he can do to be friendly and warm during those first two months is encouraged.

"For the next two months that he visits, the main goal is to get a Bible study in that home. Every Saturday is used to push this strongly—of course without being offensive. It is an all-out effort. Out of the ten or so homes he has worked with, an average captain can schedule two to four Bible studies, sometimes more. We have teachers trained and ready to teach them. That becomes the primary purpose of our bus ministry. You see, when the captains hand in their weekly report, I don't ask how many children they brought or how many new homes they visited, but how many home Bible studies they signed up."

Steve considered this for a moment then asked, "What do you do with the parents who refuse to take a home Bible study?"

"Well, we still pick up the children for as long as they will come; however, the route captain no longer visits them every Saturday. Instead, the captain finds another eight to twelve homes to bring children from and visit each week, and the four-month process is repeated."

"Isn't that somewhat cold-hearted, dropping the parents that way after four months?"

"We don't drop them. We just begin to work on them with a different approach. If one method is not working, it doesn't make sense to keep on using it. We now place these parents on our church mailing list. They receive our church bulletin in the mail each month along with any revival fliers or special-service announcements. We also assign the Sunday school teacher to visit these unsaved parents each quarter as long as the child is still coming. Our telephone committee will call them and invite them to any special services. As long as their children come, we still have a fair chance to reach those parents.

"Actually, Steve, we are trying to obey the Lord's command. Remember the parable Jesus taught concerning the servant who invited folks to the marriage supper? Talking to some people about God is like talking to an old, deaf mule. They are simply uninterested in salvation, or a Bible study, or anything else. When that's the case, Jesus said to go into the highways and byways and find those who are interested. After four months of constant witnessing, the bus workers have a pretty good idea if that parent is open to truth or not. You will not win everybody. I would prefer that our bus workers reach out and find new people who are hungry for God, instead of being tied to a handful of parents who are decidedly not."

"But aren't you ignoring little Johnny?" Steve persisted. "You forget that children have a soul too!"

"No, we're not ignoring Johnny, because we still pick him up each week. Truthfully, we are doing more to see him saved than before. Since our teachers can now handle the size of their classes, they can give more personal attention and teach with a greater burden. Then, once a month, we have a Holy Ghost Sunday."

"Holy Ghost Sunday?"

"It's the way we evangelize our Sunday school. On the first Sunday of each month, every class, from primaries to adults, teaches a lesson with one focus in mind—to give an altar call at the end. All the teachers fast and pray the week before. Then, for that one week, the teachers teach with an evangelistic emphasis, asking God to reach the children's hearts. After the lesson, the last fifteen minutes of each class are given to seeking for the Holy Ghost. Since we started the monthly Holy Ghost Sunday, hardly a month goes by without several bus children receiving the Holy Ghost. When little Johnny receives the Holy Ghost, I or my assistant will go see Mr. and Mrs. Jones to explain water baptism. It's a rare occasion that we don't get a Bible study as a result."

Tommy Keller could see real interest burning in the young man's eyes. "So if I started up my bus again," Steve replied slowly, "I'd only need about ten homes to pick up children from."

"That's," Tommy interrupted, "so that your captain can stop at each home and be friendly and have time to talk with the parents. With too many homes, he doesn't have time for the personal attention needed. Also, it's possible to put more than one captain on a bus. Each bus has three captains assigned it. The bus driver picks up children from three sets of ten homes."

Steve nodded his head in approval. "The combination of Parentreach bus ministry and a monthly Holy Ghost Sunday looks like a powerful plan for winning souls through the Sunday school, both children and adults!"

Tommy returned a wide smile. "Our results show at least fifteen families saved off our eight routes in the last two years."

"Where did you get the idea?" Steve inquired.

"It grew as the brainchild of one of our annual departmental planning retreats," Tommy replied.

Elder Keller, silent till now, glanced first at Steve

then back to his son. "Oh no, you did it now. You shouldn't have mentioned the planning retreat unless you also plan to explain what it is. I know this young man; he doesn't let anything slip by."

Steve grinned back at both of them. "You read my mind, Elder. This makes the third time you've mentioned the retreat. If it can produce ideas like the last one, I want to know about it."

Tommy glanced appealingly at his father. "Go ahead," the senior Keller told his son. "You spilled the beans; you clean them up."

"I See Where I've Gone Wrong"

Just then, their lunch came. The special that day was an eight-ounce New York with all the trimmings. The smell of the juicy, charbroiled steak was fabulous. Tommy waited until they prayed and started eating. As he carefully cut his steak, he glanced up at Steve. "Has Dad outlined what he calls the four-part planning system?"

"No, sir, he just finished talking about organization, job descriptions, and stuff."

"Well, this should tie right in. In my opinion, this is the most important part of Dad's entire concept of church growth. Without this, everything else is just another program, and the Lord knows we've had our fill of programs.

"You see, Steve, once a pastor has designed his organizational structure and selected his directors, he then needs a system to motivate, manage, and supervise them. Many pastors can delegate positions, yet few know how to keep directors excited, encouraged, and accountable for their responsibilities. That's why their organization usually crumbles. With the four-part planning system, you get maximum motivation and management, with a minimum amount of mess. Now, try saying that three times real fast."

Steve looked at Elder Keller and groaned.

The old man couldn't help but grin as Tommy continued. "The first of the four-part system is called the annual departmental planning retreat. This is known as the *plan development* stage. The second part is the departmental one-year plans, which requires *plan organization* from each department director. The third part is your monthly planning council, which is called the *plan implementation* stage, and the last part is your weekly departmental tag-in, which includes *plan accountability*. Now, does that explain everything?"

Steve looked puzzled, then rolled his eyes in mock disgust. "Yeah, sure. Now say it in English." He glanced at Elder Keller, "Does your son always ramble on this way?"

The old man and his son shared a broad smile. "What Tommy said is true, Steve," Elder Keller inserted, "and quite easy to understand. Let him explain the annual planning retreat first."

"Ten years ago," Tommy continued, "while still pastoring in Kentucky, I averaged about 450 in Sunday school. We had completely filled up our old building and had no room to expand, so we bought some land south of town and started to build. Money was tight then because we had recently started our Christian school. We couldn't afford a turnkey job, so we did almost all the construction ourselves. We often ran out of money and had to stop.

"Well, for that and other reasons, it took almost three

years to build the new facility. During that time, our Sunday school averages dropped from 450 to 370. You see Steve, every church has a natural loss rate: deaths, backsliding, move-outs, and so forth. This is called the attrition rate. It averages ten to twenty percent each year for most churches. If you're going to grow, you must exceed this loss rate with new converts. If you don't, your church will decline."

Steve cut in. "So that's why I've seen folks saved, but still had no numerical growth. All I did was equal my attrition rate."

"Precisely. If you want to grow, you must have more come in than go out. That only makes sense. Because we had to put every spare moment of our time and energy into the new facility, we had no time left for outreach, and we declined. The natural attrition rate took its toll. Even after we completed the sanctuary, the next year's average was only 374, almost no growth. I was sorely disappointed, for I had expected our growth to skyrocket.

"Well, Richard Tallor assisted me then, so we got together and evaluated our situation. We decided that the problem lay with the various outreach ministries. They were stagnant. We needed something to motivate them, get them excited, give them new ideas, and respark their vision. The solution lay, we felt, in using the planning retreat concept. Dad had already seen great results with this here in Ellisburg.

"That November we rented a lodge up on Lake Spartan, about one hour's drive from the church. All the department heads went up on Friday evening. After settling in, we prayed, had a little discussion, then went to bed. The next morning we rose early, fixed breakfast, had devotions, and began to talk—and talk we did.

"We discussed as a group how each department, ministry, and outreach might be improved. We examined problems, asked questions, and developed solutions. We prayed, we reviewed, we evaluated, we planned, and then we prayed some more. By that evening, we had formulated a strategy that we felt could help us grow.

"Now, the plan was good. It definitely gave us some positive direction. But the effect it had on my directors was even better—they got excited! Boy, you should have seen them! You could see the fire in their eyes and feel the excitement in their voice. Their enthusiasm was contagious, too; it spread to my whole church.

"We put the plan into effect the following year and saw good growth. Our average rose from 374 to 488. The next year we had another planning retreat with even better results—we averaged 593 that year. And every year since, up until I came and took Dad's church, we had a planning retreat, and each year we continued to grow. Here, let me show you."

Tommy Keller took a napkin and wrote:[1]

Year 1 450
Year 2 . . . . 415 —building program
                              started
Year 3 370
Year 4 . . . . 374 —first planning retreat
Year 5 488
Year 6 593
Year 7 640
Year 8 727

After studying the figures Tommy had written, Steve looked up, his eyes eager.

"Wow! You jumped by almost one hundred each year. If possible, I'd like to use the same plan you developed in my church. If it worked for you, then it ought to work for me."

Tommy shook his head. "No, Steve, it most likely won't. What helped me won't necessarily help you. Our churches are different in size, problems, and personalities. I don't mind showing you the ideas; however, you need your own retreat to develop your own strategies so that you can overcome the problems that keep you from growing."

Steve nodded his head resolutely. He could see the wisdom in that. He knew that many of the problems and frustrations he experienced were unique to his church and situation. He simply had to tackle each problem one by one. He also knew he could not hope to solve them by himself. He had to have the help of his department heads. Surely the planning retreat concept would help them find the answers just as it had done for Brother Keller.

Elder Keller now spoke, interrupting Steve's thoughts. "Steve, you will see three major benefits as a result of having your own retreat. The first is the enthusiasm and excitement it will create within your leaders. If your church is cold—and a cold church is like cold butter; it never spreads very well—then build a fire of enthusiasm in the hearts of your directors. I preached once that enthusiasm is nothing but faith with a tin can tied to its tail. That's true! If your department heads catch your vision, then they'll shout it from the pulpit to the pew. Your directors can achieve almost anything if they get excited about it. Build a fire under them and the fire will spread. A planning retreat builds that fire.

"Secondly, I find that people get most excited about what they develop, what they dream, and what they plan. That's what the retreat does; it gets them involved in the planning. And that's the next benefit you will find: their commitment to involvement. When they help develop the improvements and plans, they possess a strong desire to see them succeed. After all, the plan is partly their baby too."

Key Concept Four

**Thou shalt inspire thy people
to labor in harmony, dream in
unity, and think creatively.**

Steve had turned over the paper place mat on the table and was writing furiously. "I knew I should have brought my notebook," he grumbled, "or better yet, a tape recorder. My hand hurts." He glanced up at the old pastor. "And the third benefit?"

The old pastor paused for a moment to let the young man catch up. "The third benefit is the greatest and is truly the main reason for having a retreat. That's to allow the Holy Ghost to direct their minds to develop new ideas and solutions to difficult problems. I saw more outstanding ideas come as a result of the planning retreat than by any other method.

"Now, I've known some men to be on such an ego trip as to think the only good ideas are their ideas—that blowing out another man's candle will make their own candle shine brighter. Such men always pastor small churches. The greatest leaders always develop the talents and abilities of people whose gifts are greater than their own. Proverbs says, 'The ear of the wise seeketh knowledge,' or as one translation renders, 'is open to new ideas.' God put within the human mind the one ability that separates us from all other life: creative ingenuity and the power to reason. The greatest resource for growth that you have, Steve, is the minds of your people. Many of them will have talents that are far greater than your own in some areas. These talents and ideas will come to the surface in the kind of atmosphere that the retreat provides. The retreat is simply one, giant brainstorming session under the direction of the Spirit."

Steve paused in writing. "Couldn't some suggestions or ideas be premature or even harmful?"

"Yes, I sometimes have to redirect the discussion for just that reason, and of course, I explain that before we start. But don't be too quick to judge an idea. I read once of an irate banker who told an inventor to remove 'that toy' from his office. That toy was the telephone. Why, it hasn't even been ten years since Hewlett-Packard, the electronics corporation, called a small home computer that an employee built 'a waste of time.' Because of its response, the employee quit and started his own company. Today that computer is known as the Apple.

"Many of the best and most effective outreach programs in our church came from seed thoughts sown at our annual retreats. So use caution, son. A new idea is

126

delicate. It can be killed by a sneer or yawn, strangled by a frown, or stabbed by the careless remark 'It will never work.' Your directors' creativity is one of those things that comes under the 'use it or lose it' category."

Steve had paused in his writing, chewing on the end of his pencil. "You know, Elder, it's funny how we pastors will go from one extreme to another. If we know almost nothing about a job or position, we will give it to a person, tell them to do it, and provide no help, no training, no job description—nothing. But if the job is in an area we consider ourselves competent in, we'll want the director to do it our way or no way, with no flexibility for personal creativity. I can see right now where I've gone wrong in both my Sunday School Department and my Youth Department. The Sunday School Department I just let go, and the Youth Department I bound into a rigid mold. Both directors want to quit." Steve sighed heavily. "Whoever said truth hurts knew what it meant."

Dreams Can Come True
Tommy leaned back and stretched. "Actually," he said with a yawn, "the retreat can be summed up in the words of Solomon when he said, 'Plans fail when there is no council, but succeed when counselors are many.' "[2]

Steve looked from father to son. "All right, you've convinced me. I'll have a retreat. When's the best time to plan it?"

This time Tommy answered. "Well, we just had our annual retreat. We always schedule it in late October or early November so we can get a head start on the new year. However, if you want it to be successful, you will probably need to wait until January because of several things you'll need to do first—developing your organization, writing job descriptions, designing departmental reports, and so on."

"Won't waiting until January lower its effectiveness?" Steve questioned.

"Oh no. I've seen pastors hold them in mid summer. What you don't ever want to do is to just skip it. The four-part planning process will not work without a retreat first. Having a retreat in January or February and then another in November won't hurt. In fact, two retreats each year—if you can afford it—would be great. Many large corporations have executive retreats once a quarter."

"How do I go about planning it?" Steve asked.

"Well, the best way is to take a three-day vacation," Tommy answered.

"You mean with my directors?"

"No, by yourself."

"But why?"

"To dream."

"Dream?"

"Sure," Tommy said simply. "I always try to get off by myself for several days to pray and dream before the retreat. I use what I call a five-year dream sheet." (See figure 7.) "On the left side of the page I write down all of the dreams that I would like to see become reality in the next five years. I usually start with number goals. Has Dad shown you the five-year numerical goal plan—the one using the progressive progression concept? Good. Each year I check my goals. If I greatly exceed or fall short of my goals in Sunday school, adult members, or new converts, then I may want to readjust and fill out another five-year numerical goal worksheet.

"Then, I consider each department one at a time as to how it might be improved or expanded within the next five years. I also look at my facilities and buildings and list any five-year improvements. New ministries or outreaches are also considered. Three years ago, I dreamed of starting a cell ministry. This next year it will become reality. We will also break ground on our new sanctuary next March. Planning began four years ago.

"After I have written down each dream on the left, then on the right side I put my goal for this year that will put me one step closer to seeing that dream come true. Dreams, Steve, are what I would like to see happen, by faith. Goals are what, with the Lord's help, I am going to do. Many men dream, Steve, and keep right on sleeping. To grow you must wake up and turn dreams into reality."

"So," Steve injected, "it's the goals you develop from your five-year dream sheet that you take to the retreat?"

"Exactly. Each year I review my dream sheet from last year and make a new one for this year. Some dreams become unrealistic because of changing circumstances. But if that dream is still burning within, I rewrite it on this year's dream sheet. A dream may take five years before it's fully realized. Others may take only one or two. Yet each year I do what I can to see each dream fulfilled. Make sense?"

"Yes, sir," Steve nodded. "I sort of did that in the past, but I never wrote it down. When you neglect to write it down, it kind of . . . well, fades."

Tommy nodded his agreement. "By not writing it down, you will also fail to work on it each year. For example, starting a cell ministry appeared too great a task

129

Figure 7

Five-Year Dream Sheet

For the Year of 1989

(A new dream sheet should be completed each year)

(PAGE ONE)

What Quality Improvements I would like to see accomplished within the next five years:	What I can do this year toward the fulfillment of this goal.	Starting & Ending Date
(Try to do something on each goal each year. Remember: the longest journey is achieved by taking the first step.)		
1. BEGIN FOUR PART PLANNING SYSTEM	DO ALL THIS YEAR	1-89
2. START VISITOR FOLLOW-UP PROGRAM	DO ALL THIS YEAR	1-89
3. START CHRISTIAN SCHOOL	A. POLL PARENTS TO SEE INTEREST B. VISIT 3 SCHOOLS IN AREA	2-89 / 5-89
4. START CHURCH GROWTH SPIRAL MINISTRY	DO ALL THIS YEAR	3-89
5. BEGIN A BOY SCOUT MINISTRY IN OUR CHURCH	A. SEND FOR INFORMATION B. HAVE BRO. TEEL VISIT A CHURCH THAT HAS A CHAPTER GOING	4-89 / 5-89
6. HAVE A NEW CHURCH BUILT BY 1991	HAVE SITE PLANS DRAWN UP THIS YEAR	6-89
7. BEGIN WEEKLY LEADERSHIP TRAINING CLASS ON FRI. NIGHT	DO ALL THIS YEAR	7-89
8. PURCHASE NEW PHOTOCOPIER	RAISE 50% OF PURCHASE PRICE FOR DOWN PAYMENT	7-89 / 9-89
9. HAVE AN "ENROLL TO GROW" CRUSADE	DO ALL THIS YEAR	8-89
10. REMODEL FELLOWSHIP HALL	HAVE BRO. JACOB DRAW UP PLANS & GET ESTIMATE	8-89 / 10-89
11. PURCHASE CHURCH COMPUTER	HAVE BRO. DAVIS REVIEW & PRICE 3 SYSTEMS	9-89 / 10-89
12. HAVE A "TOTAL CHURCH CAMP" IN MOUNTAINS IN 1990	A. LOOK FOR GOOD LOCATION B. MAKE RESERVATIONS	9-89 / 10-89
13. PURCHASE 6 MORE BUSES BY 1992	A. PURCHASE 2 THIS YEAR B. HAVE BRO. DOE LOOKING	10-89 / 12-89
14. START A "CELL MINISTRY" BY 1991	A. VISIT 2 CHURCHES THAT HAVE ONE B. READ 3 BOOKS ON SUBJECT	11-89 / 12-89
15. START A BRANCH CHURCH IN GLENWOOD	A. START EXTENSION S.S. THERE THIS YEAR B. HAVE BRO. THOMAS LOOK FOR A SITE	12-89

"I can do all things through Christ who strengthens me."

- Apostle Paul

130

all at once. However, flying to California to see it working and reading three books on cell groups that first year
appeared a whole lot easier. So that became the first
year's goal and also a step in the right direction."

Steve made a few more notes on his place mat, then
looked at Elder Keller, who had been sitting quietly listening. "Can I borrow your place mat, Elder? I've run out
of paper."

As he spoke, the waitress walked up and began stack-
ing dishes to clear the table.

"Ma'am," Elder Keller asked the waitress, "do you
have any note paper this young man could borrow? He's
about ready to write on the tablecloth."

The waitress's eyebrows shot up. "I can't think of any,
sir. How about a paper place mat? You could write on the
back . . ."

They all three laughed. "That sounds fine," the old
man grinned. "At least it will be clean."

Steve took the new place mat, then spoke to the elder
minister. "Brother Keller, I don't understand something.
While at the retreat, do I need to follow some kind of a
schedule, or do I just throw out topics for discussion?"

The old pastor looked at his son. "I'm going to let
Tommy explain that. He's doing fine so far."

"I can do better than that, Steve," Tommy replied.
"Let me show you." He reached over and took several
pages out of his coat pocket. "Just this morning I met
with Jo Ann to review the plans from our retreat, and
I still have the agenda with me."

Like A Mighty, Moving Army
He spread out the papers on the table. (See Figure 8.)

131

Figure 8
1988 Annual Planning Retreat Agenda

Friday Evening October 14

8:00– 8:30   Prayer & pastor's vision

8:30– 9:00   GENERAL TOPICS—Bro. Tom Keller
   1. Departmental one-year plans—due date
   2. Monthly planning council—set dates
   3. Weekly tag-in time
   4. Leadership training topics
   5. 1989 retreat date
   6. Pastor's vacation

9:00– 9:30   VISITOR FOLLOW-UP DEPARTMENT—
Bro. Barentine
   1. How to get more people involved in visitor follow-up
   2 Visitor follow-up training date
   3. New visitors welcome brochure

9:30–10:00   MUSIC DEPARTMENT—Bro. Thomas
   1. How to get youth more involved in music ministry.
   2. Singspiration
   3. Christmas caroling outreach
   4. Choir clinic in May

10:00–12:00   Free time or "snooze"

Saturday October 15

7:30– 8:30   Breakfast

8:30– 9:00   Prayer

9:00– 9:50   YOUTH DEPARTMENT—Bro. Johnson
   1. How to increase the youth service attendance
   2. Youth revival
   3. Bible quizzing ministry
   4. Youth outings

                  5. Fund-raising ideas
                  6. Youth outreach involvement ideas

9:50–10:00   **Break**

10:00–10:50   **SUNDAY SCHOOL DEPARTMENT—**
                  Bro. Powell
                  1. Teacher training—needs & date
                  2. Children's church—location & facilities
                  3. Buzz Groups: Christmas, Pentecost Sunday,
                     Easter, & fall thrust programs
                  4. Parentreach concept for bus ministry

10:50–11:00   **Break**

11:00–12:00   **OUTREACH DEPARTMENT—Bro. Davies**
                  1. Spiral promotion ideas for 1989
                  2. Saturday door-knocking dates & ideas
                  3. New tract rack
                  4. Starting a jail ministry
                  5. C.C.C.—getting more involvement

12:00– 1:00   **Lunch and free time**

1:00– 1:50   **LADIES AUXILIARY—Sis. Davis**
                  1. Is a family and marriage seminar possible?
                  2. Mother's Memorial 1989
                  3. Starting a food barrel for needy families
                  4. Dates and plans:
                     *Christmas banquet
                     *Labor Day and Memorial Day—1989
                     picnics

1:50– 2:00   **Break**

2:00– 2:50   **HOME BIBLE STUDY—Bro. Hall**
                  1. Promoting H.B.S. in the church better!
                  2. How to get more H.B.S.
                  3. Annual H.B.S.
                  4. Using the Quest survey

2:50– 3:00   **Break**

3:00– 3:50   **NEW CONVERTS DEPARTMENT—**
                  Sis. Duncan

                 1. Expanding our new convert training class
                 2. How to improve new convert friendship development
                 3. First night counseling—Tape & Booklet
                 4. Quarterly new convert socials—ideas & dates

3:50– 4:00   Break

4:00– 4:30   PRAYER MINISTRY DEPARTMENT— Sis. Perry
                 1. Annual prayer revival
                 2. January week of prayer & quarterly prayer chains
                 3. Starting a prayer library
                 4. Prayer hotline

4:30– 5:30   MEN'S MINISTRIES DEPARTMENT— Bro. Tullison
                 1. How to get constant volunteers for yard maintenance
                 2. Repair Projects—north wall of educational building
                 3. Usher & hostess training
                 4. Men's fishing trip & father/son camp-out
                 5. Men's prayers breakfasts—dates & topics

5:30– 6:30   Dinner

6:30– 7:20   PROMOTIONS DEPARTMENT—Sis. Moore
                 1. New advertising methods—Yellow Pages & newspaper
                 2. Monthly bulletin—any ideas?
                 3. Public service announcements
                 4. Citywide mail-out for crusade—layout ideas.

7:20– 7:30   Break

7:30– 8:00   CHRISTIAN SCHOOL DEPARTMENT— Bro. Thomas
                 1. Computer training for next year
                 2. School choir trip
                 3. Annual God & Country program ideas

4. New sports equipment

8:00–11:00   Free time or "snooze"

Sunday, October 16

Pack-up and leave in time to be at the church
by 9:00 a.m.!

"As you can see, we always begin with prayer and devotion. Next you see a section called General Topics. Many of these are items off my dream sheet that I wanted to introduce and discuss. Then beneath each department are three or four subjects. These topics are a combination of the directors' ideas and also my own. We ask ourselves, What could I do to my department or ministry to improve it or make it better? This is important because I've yet to see a perfect department or program. If we can add something to help its effectiveness, let's do it.

"You see, Steve, I love beans and cornbread. However, if I ate beans and cornbread every night for dinner I'd soon grow tired of it. The same is true of your directors. If they only do the same thing year in and year out within their departments, they soon grow tired of it. Their ministry becomes stagnant and their excitement fades. After a while, they only do their job out of obligation, not from a burden. Then they quit. What they leave for the next director is a bunch of problems and frustrations that were never solved. And that is something else we talk about at the retreat: What am I doing now that's having problems or is not working properly? Problems will hinder a department's progress and effectiveness and add to the director's discouragement."

"How," Steve asked, "did you get these subjects from

the directors? Did you meet with each director individually?"

"That's exactly what I did," Tommy answered. "About a month before the retreat, I had Jo Ann call all directors and schedule an hour with each one. A few met with me during the day, but the rest required two evenings and a Saturday. It's a once-a-year, one-on-one situation. During that meeting I review and update their job description, discuss results of the past year, listen to any ideas for improvement, and express my own proposals and suggestions. The ideas and problems that are most crucial are then placed on the agenda for discussion by the entire council. The council will brainstorm as a group and work out a plan or solution. Of course, neither I nor the department director is obligated to follow all ideas or suggestions. We pick and choose the best as needed. That is what brainstorming is all about."

"By brainstorming you mean everyone throws their ideas together to work out a plan, right?"

"Right. When you brainstorm, you try to get as many ideas as possible. I tell the directors that there's no such thing as a dumb idea. In fact, the crazier the better. It is often the crazy idea that is just the spark needed to bring a great idea. All negative judgment is suspended. Hitchhiking and tying ideas together are encouraged. Everybody must participate."

"Sounds like fun."

"It is. The directors look forward to the retreat each year. When we first started, everyone paid his own expenses. Now that the church is larger, it carries the bill. It's somewhat of a reward to the directors for a job well done. But don't let finances keep you from having your own. Do what you can and ask the directors to pay the rest. Many smaller churches rent one cabin, put all the women upstairs, men downstairs, and go slumber-party style. Our first year was like that and everyone had a blast. Now, let me give you a list of suggestions I've learned through experience that will make the retreat go much better."[3]

When Steve finished writing the suggestions, he leaned back with a sigh. "Having a retreat is more involved than I thought. It pays to talk to someone who's done it before. I would have probably wasted several years finding out what you've told me in ten minutes."

Elder Keller shook his head. "Not wasted, Steve. Learning is never wasted. The only person who doesn't make mistakes is the one who does nothing. You are bound to make mistakes this first time around. Your second and third retreat will go even better. As your directors come to understand how it works, they will relax and participate even more. You will develop a team spirit on the council. The more you work together, the more you will accomplish."

"What do you mean by team spirit?" Steve asked.

"Up to now, Steve, your departments have probably operated as little kingdoms within themselves. This is a common problem, because every church has a limited supply of money, manpower, pastor's time, dates, and so forth. Your departments, if you are not careful, will compete against one another for these limited resources. That is not good.

"A kingdom divided against itself will not stand, and a body at war with itself will not survive. The retreat will help by binding together the directors into a single body.

Not only will they develop a burden for their department, but for their neighbor's department as well. They will see how each part of the body is important to the operation of the whole. Like an army moving together in a unified front, the work of God will push forward. When God's people get together in unity and purpose, the kingdom of darkness will be destroyed!''

"Praise God!" Steve shouted—a little too loudly, for people turned around in their seats. He ducked his head. "I mean, praise God," he whispered. "I can hardly wait to get this going!"

Tommy grinned. "Wait until you hear about the departmental one-year plans, and the monthly planning council, and the—"

"Wait a minute!" Elder Keller exclaimed, interrupting him. "Don't get him started on that yet, or we'll be here all afternoon."

"Yikes," Tommy said, looking at his watch. "It's two o'clock! I've work to do, folks. Time to head back to the church. If you'll excuse me . . .''

"Sure," Steve said, as he reached out and picked up the meal ticket. "You two split the tip, and I'll pay the tab. No argument," he commanded as both men started to protest. "Muzzle not the ox, and all that stuff. You've earned yourself a meal. Let your student pay for this one."

"Now he's calling us an ox," Elder Keller growled as they pushed back their chairs. "This younger generation gives you no respect."

Steve only laughed as they made their way to the door.

Chapter Six

Pursuing Goals Together

When the trio arrived back at the church, Tommy Keller excused himself to take care of some business at the Christian school. After leading Steve back through the large double doors, Elder Keller stopped at the church office before returning to Tommy's study.

"I want to show you our departmental one-year plans," he explained to Steve. "The one-year plan is a critical step in the management process that Tommy explained to you. I'll ask Jo Ann to run off a sample from each department."

Steve watched as Jo Ann began making the duplicates on the office copier. "Boy, a photocopier is something my church could sure use," he said as he admired the new Xerox spitting out one page after another. "Only I can't make up my mind whether to get that first or a computer. A computer sure would be handy for word processing and filing and the like."

The old pastor glanced back with a cocked eyebrow. "Steer clear of the computer, son, until you absolutely need one.[1] They are extremely useful; however, some types of computers are difficult to learn and use. I've seen too many churches where they sit and gather dust or become glorified paperweights. Yet you're right about the other. A good-quality photocopier is one of the wisest investments a church can make. Once purchased, you'll wonder how you ever did without it."

The young man grinned ruefully. "Sure, but a computer sounds like more fun. Whoever heard of playing Pac-Man on a copier?"

Jo Ann finished running the requested material and returned the originals to the file. She set the stack on the marble counter, still warm from the copier. The first one-year plan was from the Sunday School Department. The typed page was neatly laid out in three bold sections: Numerical Goals, Quality Improvement Goals, and Annual Activities. Various dates followed each item. Steve picked it up to study more carefully. (See figure 9.)

Figure 9
SUNDAY SCHOOL ONE-YEAR PLAN
Apostolic Tabernacle
John Powell–Director

NUMERICAL GOALS

1. S.S. average by end of 1988   790
2. Bus ministry average by end of 1988   270
3. Bus ministry Bible studies from   40
   Parentreach
4. Class goals:

Adult	240	Jr. Girls	120	Sr. High	50
Pri. Boys	100	Jr. High	45	Pri. Girls	65
Jr. Boys	140	Nursery	30		

QUALITY IMPROVEMENT GOALS

Completion Date

1. Have a monthly Holy Ghost Sunday to include an altar call in each class. — 1–3

2. Start Parentreach to reach the parents of bus children. — February

3. Begin Sunday morning teachers prayer at 9:15. — 3–6

4. Establish teachers standard of excellence. Post names and pictures each month. — April

5. Have a three-night teachers training seminar. — 4–12

6. Start a comprehensive absentee follow-up program. — 5–2

7. Fix up S.S. office (paint, panel, carpet). — October

ANNUAL ACTIVITIES

1. EASTER OUTREACH Goal: 1000 — 4–3
   *Drama: "We Must See Jesus"

2. PENTECOST SUNDAY Goal: 900 — 5–22
   *Enroll to Grow drive

3. THRUST SUNDAY Goal: 900 — 9–11
   *Team Reach S.S. drive

4. CHRISTMAS PROGRAM Goal: 850 — 12–4
   *Total class pageant/drama/musical

141

"What's the reason for each department turning in one of these, Elder? I thought you took care of all this at the retreat."

"In some ways, Steve, that's true. Almost everything on the departmental one-year plan we discussed and approved at the retreat and added to the master calendar of the church. However, the primary purpose of having a department hand in a one-year plan is not to just get a lot of dates written down, but rather to solve a serious complication that arises as a result of the retreat. The one-year plan eliminates this problem quite well."

"What problem?"

"That of your directors trying to do too much too quickly. Remember, the retreat will benefit you in three ways: enthusiasm, committed involvement, and new ideas. That can add up to trouble if not handled properly. Your directors will want to come back and immediately put all these great ideas into effect, one program on top of another. With eight or ten departments all pushing three or four new programs each, all at the same time, you won't have growth; you'll have a mess."

Key Concept Five

**Thou shalt plan thy work
effectively, keeping in mind thy
ultimate aim and purpose.**

Steve's mouth twitched with amusement. "You know, Elder, I know exactly what you mean. When I first graduated from Bible college I had a lot of zeal and not a whole lot of brains. When my pastor asked me to come back and help him get their outreach going, I went back to my home church determined to turn the world upside down. I drew up what I thought was a great plan and put it on his desk. If I can remember right, it went something like this: in January I wanted to start visitor follow-up, home Bible study, and bus ministry. In February I planned new converts classes, door-knocking teams, altar worker classes, and a Sunday school revival. In March I scheduled a citywide crusade, campus evangelism, street services, ethnic ministries . . .''

"Hold it, hold it!" Elder Keller laughed, waving his arms in feigned desperation. "You can't be serious. Not all at once!"

"Yep. I intended to do it all. Thankfully, my pastor had more wisdom than that. He didn't crush my excitement; he directed it. He looked at my plan and said, 'Looks good, Steve. Tell you what; get visitor follow-up started, and when that's flowing well, we'll begin a home Bible study ministry. When that's operating smoothly, we'll launch the bus ministry, and so on.' 'Oh, it will work just this way, Pastor!', I told him," Steve paused, a toothy grin stretching from ear to ear. "And by the end of that first year, I had two of them going!"

The old pastor threw back his head and roared with laughter.

"You sound exactly like an assistant I had one time," he said as he wiped tears from the corners of his eyes. He put his hand on Steve's shoulder. "So you learned a valuable lesson, didn't you? It takes time to begin a new ministry or outreach. You can't turn a ship around in an instant. Do you see, Steve, that your directors will come back from your annual planning retreat and try to do exactly that? Few people can work effectively on more than one project at a time. For precisely that reason, I require each director to turn in a one-year plan. It forces them to schedule their activities and goals carefully. I make this plan due two or three weeks after the retreat. It's made up of three parts. Look at your sample for Sunday school.

"The first part is called Numerical Goals. Our Sunday school director set a goal to average 790 by the end of this year, which he's almost reached. His bus ministry has a goal to obtain home Bible studies and riders, and each class has a goal. Now, every department may not need numerical goals. For example, the men's ministries or the Christian school may not. Yet every department does have room for improvement, so they all should have something under Quality Improvement Goals. Now, as I said, most topics listed here we discussed at the retreat. Many of these are the ideas that developed from our brainstorming. Now I need each director to put everything in writing and tell me when they purpose to do it. Remember, a goal is not a goal until a date is put upon it.

"I also tell them," the old pastor continued, "to spread their quality improvement goals throughout the year. I advocate the double trouble rule: If you figure it will take one month to complete a project, then give yourself two months, for it always takes twice as long to do something as you think. They are not allowed to start a new project until they've finished the previous one, so all goals should be placed in priority order. This gives them a strong feeling of direction and purpose. They also accomplish more."

Steve studied the sample one-year plan, nodding his

head as Elder Keller spoke. "I can see why this is so crucial, Elder. This way each director knows what he is to do and when he is to do it. I'm sure it also helps you know when you can schedule revivals and things."

"Yes and no," the retired minister replied pointedly. "When God speaks to me that it's time for a revival, we have revival. The departments reschedule their plans to fit with God's plans. I let the directors know plainly that nothing on the calendar or the one-year plan is chiseled in stone. Every department stays flexible, and we adjust things as needed. Yet you're right; it does help me schedule other activities. That's where the third step, plan implementation, comes in. Planning is the golden chain that ties where you are now to where you want to go."

The young man wore a bewildered expression. "I thought planning was what you did at the retreat. Then you tell me I should collect one-year plans. Now you say I must plan again. You have me confused."

"It's all planning, Steve. That's why it's called a four-part planning process. As Tommy mentioned at the restaurant, effective planning is done in four stages. The first step is your retreat, where you brainstorm and develop your plans. The second step, the samples you're holding, show how those plans become organized. But the third step is your plan implementation stage—where you make it all happen. You do this at the monthly departmental council. It's one thing to talk and dream and envision. It's another thing to follow through. Failing to follow through with plans is a major reason for not growing. Plans and ideas are funny things: they don't work unless you do."

Steve still looked doubtful. "Monthly council?"

Elder Keller put his arm around the young man's shoulders. "Come on. Let's go back to Tommy's office, and I'll show you how the monthly council works."

The Monthly Planning Council

In the office, Steve sat and watched as Brother Keller flipped through the desk drawer until he located a file. From this he withdrew a page, handing it to Steve.

"This is one of our recent council agendas. As I told you, the council is made up of each department leader. It's scheduled once a month and held on an off-church night. It's here that we work out detailed plans for the ideas developed at our annual retreat."

Steve read through the agenda carefully. (See figure 10.)

"When are your council meetings?"

"They're scheduled on the first Tuesday of every month. At the retreat we go through the entire year and mark all monthly council dates on our calendars. Occasionally a date gets bumped to another night or week, although not very often. A church should choose a day and time that works best for everyone and stick to it. That way your directors can plan in advance to attend.

And notice I said every month. Some churches have tried to meet with their directors only once a quarter. We tried that and it doesn't work—too much to plan. It turned into nothing more than a calendar session with no time to work on details. Planning involves more than just setting dates. We always ask ourselves several questions about every agenda item: where it's going to be, who's to be involved, how much it will cost, who's in charge, how we will promote it, and so on. We are not so much developing plans as we are implementing plans—making them happen. Look at the discussion items under each department. Most of these topics came directly off that department's one-year plan."

Figure 10
Monthly Planning Council Agenda
Apostolic Tabernacle
For the Month of August 1988

Date: Tuesday, August 2, 1988
Leadership Development Assignment: Tape #3—Leadership series

Schedule
7:30–7:45	Prayer
7:45–8:15	Leadership Development
8:15–9:30	Planning & Reports

Topics For Discussion	Date
1. Sunday School Department	
*Fall attendance drive	8–21
*Begin Sunday morning teachers training	9–18
*Purchase new bus	9–30
2. Youth Department	
*Youth crusade	8–12
*Youth Revival with Bro. Massengale	8–25
*Youth trip	9–17
3. Outreach Department	
*New tract rack	8–19
*Spirit of Freedom promotion service	9–4
*Saturday door-knocking teams	10–22

4. Visitor Follow-Up Department
   *Follow-up training seminar   8–5
   *Print visitor packet   10–20
5. Home Bible Study Department
   *Annual H.B.S. seminar   9–8
   *Bible study Promotion night   9–25
   *Quest survey teams   9–26
6. New Converts Department
   *Fall new-convert potluck   8–9
   *Visiting backsliders   9–13
7. Music Department
   *New portable sound system   8–20
   *Annual singspiration   9–30
8. Men's Fellowship Department
   *Men's prayer breakfast   8–13
   *Men's prayer meeting   8–22
9. Ladies Auxiliary Department
   *Revised church-cleaning list   9–1
   *Ladies Day—getting visitors   9–11

Key Concept Six

**Thou shalt not abandon thy people
as they pursue their goals
but shalt meet with them consistently
to plan in unity of purpose.**

"That department did all this in August?"

"No, Steve, look at the dates on the right. At the monthly council, we always look ahead at least three months. The August council, which you have, planned not only for August but also for September and October. The September council planned for October, November, and December. By always looking three months ahead, we are able to stay on top of all that is happening. And since our planning is much more detailed, we can more readily identify potential problems."

"Now I see," Steve injected. "That way every item on the one-year plan appears on the agenda three times: the first time is three months before it happens and you can do long-range planning, the second time you would probably do intermediate planning, and the final time is to do last-minute planning."

Brother Keller crinkled into a broad smile. "Hey, you catch on quick! What Jo Ann, our secretary, will do is take out each department's one-year plan each month. Any quality-improvement goals or department activities that fall within those three months, she will list as topics of discussion. That's why I require every item on the one-year plans to be dated. If it has no date, it will never appear on the monthly council agenda."

Steve nodded his head thoughtfully. "All right. Now, what's this part at the top labeled Schedule?"

"That's the basic time schedule we follow. We always pray together as a group for about fifteen minutes. Then we give time for instruction—leadership training—where we teach leadership principles to the directors. Leaders are not born, Steve, they are developed. Your directors will only be leaders if you train them. We always set aside a half hour for good, straightforward instruction. After that, each director hands in a report."

"Report?" Steve queried with a scowl. "Why the

149

paper work? It only bogs down an operation!"

"You're exactly right, excessive paper work will harm any organization. You want as little as necessary, but unfortunately, some is necessary. We ask each director to hand in a brief written report at every monthly council. Let me show you."

Placing Accountability
with the Responsibility

Elder Keller stood and walked slowly to the desk. Picking up the telephone he punched the intercom. "Sister Jo Ann? Could you bring us a sample of each department's report? Thank you."

The old man eased down into the desk chair and leaned back with a sigh, slowly rubbing his forehead.

"You feeling bad, sir?" Steve asked with a look of concern.

"Oh, it's nothing really," the old pastor replied lightly, a smile playing at the corners of his mouth. "A slight headache. I'm not used to staying up with you younguns."

The door opened and Jo Ann came in, handing Brother Keller a file folder. "Would you two care for some coffee?" she asked cheerfully.

"Hey, just what I need," Elder Keller exclaimed. "How about you, son?"

"Sure, with a touch of cream."

As Jo Ann departed, Elder Keller opened the file and thumbed through it. "This is one of our reports from the Sunday School Department," he said as he handed it to Steve. "All the monthly reports are designed specifically for each department. When I first started using reports, I began with a standard form that was identical for every director. It basically asked, 'What did you do last month and what are you doing next month?' I wasn't satisfied with the results.

"Generic reports brought generic answers. I couldn't tell anything specific about that department or how it was doing. Sometimes a department would go along for months, appearing to be busy, yet still not accomplishing anything. Remember, son, it's not how much you do that counts, but how much you get done. The bottom line for a singles ministry is not what socials are planned but how many souls are saved. The report should reflect the department's reason for existence.

"There is an old business maxim that says, *Responsibility without accountability is total futility.* Not only do the reports give me an efficient method of evaluating each department, they also help make the directors accountable for their duties. I discovered that the report does two things: first, it forces the directors to stay on top of what's happening in their departments, and second, it makes them focus upon their main purpose and objectives. Look at the Sunday school report you have. (See figure 11.)

"This report," Brother Keller continued, "zeros in on the two objectives of Sunday school. The first is numerical growth. We require all outreach-oriented departments to set number goals each year. We divide these annual goals by twelve to come up with monthly goals. The Sunday school's goal this year was to add sixty in attendance—about five people each month. So the report asks for the attendance each week and the month's average, then compares the average to the monthly goal. We do the same thing for absentees, children's church,

Figure 11

Sunday School Department Report
For the Month of July '89

A. Have you read your one-year plan this month?___Yes_____
B. Did you complete this month's leadership training assignment?___Yes___

	Week 1	Week 2	Week 3	Week 4	Week 5	Aver./ Total	Goal
S.S. Attendance	774	757	724	768	748	754	756
Absentees	32	49	82	40	58	52	50
Offerings	211.	205.	181.	233.	218.	216.	200.
Children's Church	97	101	72	115	103	104	100
Teacher's Prayer Att.	72	71	67	75	70	72	75

Number of children baptized this month (any service)_____4_____
Number of children who received the Holy Ghost this month (any service)___4___
Goal for children saved this year____80____Number saved to date___51___

Goals or Assignments Last Month	Completed? (✔)	Reason not Completed	Problem Solution
1. Order Next Qtr. Literature	✓		
2. Have Parent Sunday	✓		
3. Sunday School Picnic		Canceled	Rescheduled

Goals or assignments for next month (1-year plan)	As pastor, what can I do to assist you with these goals?
1. Fall Attendance Drive: 8-21	Need to choose team captains
2. Carpet for Children's Church	Money! ($425.00)
3.	

C. What are the results of your current outreach efforts?___Going Great!___

D. Is there anything concerning your goals or department that you need to see me about? Yes — Need New Jr. Girls Teacher bus routes, offering, and the Sunday-morning teachers prayer meeting. If we miss our goal, we stop and evaluate why, then work out a plan for improvement."

The young man interrupted excitedly. "So if attendance is down, you might plan a contest, or if the absentee count is high, your absentee follow-up system might be slipping."

"Exactly," Elder Keller said. "We pay special attention to the averages in each category. A drop in the teachers prayer meeting attendance often will precede a decline in children receiving the Holy Ghost. The second section asks how many children were baptized or received the Holy Ghost each month as a result of our Sunday school efforts. To me, this is critical because this is our second main objective."

The young man frowned, glancing up from his note taking. "I thought the Sunday school was mainly to teach the Bible to the children."

The old man nodded. "It is. Yet when you teach the Word of God properly, there should be a response. I wanted our children to be doers as well as hearers. Sunday school is the ideal environment for bringing children to the knowledge of their need for salvation. If the teachers teach with a burden, salvation will be the result."

"But in a smaller Sunday school, will children be saved every month? Won't the superintendent be continually putting down zeros on the report?"

"Well, some months will pass without any children saved. However, you shouldn't be going month after month after month with nothing except zeros. If that is the case, something should spark in both your heart and your superintendent's. That's another reason for your report: evaluation. Besides, with the monthly Holy Ghost Sunday in effect, few months will pass without results."

The young man nodded his agreement. "So the report not only allows you to evaluate their progress but makes the directors evaluate their progress as well."

"Right," the old pastor replied. "Now, the information for the next part of the report—Goals or Assignments Last Month—comes primarily off their one-year plan. Any goal on their one-year plan that was to be completed the month before should be noted here. They should also list any assignments you gave them at the previous monthly council. You will find that many things will come up as the year progresses that will need attention yet won't be on the one-year plan.

"I always tried to put these directives in writing. A basic management law states, *Never give an oral directive; always put it in writing.* So any goals that were supposed to be completed from their one-year plan and any assignments you asked them to get done go in this third section. Then they should check in the Completed column if they accomplished it. The reason anything was incomplete is put in the next column, and the proposed solution to the problem is put in the last."

"In other words," Steve said with a chuckle, "they should work out their own solutions with fear and trembling."

The elder preached laughed. "That's one way of putting it."

"And the last part? These are their goals and assignments to be worked on in the coming month?"

"You guessed it."

"Isn't the next question—As pastor, what can I do

154

to assist you with these goals—somewhat dangerous?"

"Why?"

"They might say, 'Do it for me!' "

"Hmm. . . ," Elder Keller pondered, his eyes twinkling, "hasn't happened yet, although there's always a first time. Truthfully, that's one of the most important areas on the report. It sends a powerful message to your director that says, You do your job, and I'll do all I can to help you. Some things just will not work unless the pastor lends a hand. Your directors will have no trouble filling that section up."

The young man gave another approving nod. He leafed carefully through the other reports, pausing to look at each one.

"I want to get a copy of these too, Elder. I'm sure that, like the job descriptions, they will need to be customized and retyped, yet they'll give me an example to go by."

"No problem," Elder Keller agreed, "and you're correct about retyping them. The reports should directly reflect what you have asked your directors to do in their job descriptions. By requesting information about their specific responsibilities, the reports encourage faithfulness. A powerful motivator is feedback on results. When your directors hand in their reports, Steve, always comment on the totals as good or bad. Compliment them on any goal or assignment that went well, or discuss any problems that arose. Upcoming assignments should be noted and directives given. In other words, take the report seriously. If you act as though the reports are unimportant, they will feel that their department and responsibilities are unimportant. Then, after a director hands in

155

his report and you've made comments, go over the department's agenda topics and make your plans."

Key Concept Seven

**Thou shalt require thy people to give
an account of their labors that
they be not slothful in their duties
and position.**

The elderly pastor paused, biting his lower lip in thought. "You still have room in that notebook?"

"Yes, sir."

"Good. Let me give you a list of suggestions that might make your monthly councils go better." Elder Keller listed several points one after another.[2]

When Steve finished writing, he set his pen down with a crooked grin, rubbing his hand as he spoke. "I don't know how much longer my fingers will last, Elder. But I'm not as concerned about my hand as I am my head. With all you've told me these last two days, my brain's spinning."

The old pastor cocked a bushy eyebrow. "Tired? A hardy young fellow like you? Why, when I was your age I . . ."

The Weekly Tag-In

The opening of the office door broke their conversation. Jo Ann entered carrying a tray of coffee, and right on her heels came Tommy, complaining to her loudly.

". . . that guy calls again to cancel, let me talk to him. This makes the third time he's put us off, and I'm getting tired of it."

"Problems?" Elder Keller asked his son.

Tommy's face burned red and mirrored his disgust. "Oh, it's that fellow who installed the school's new phone system. The intercom quit working three weeks ago, so we called him to fix it. He keeps calling back to say he can't make it this week and he'll come out the next. Meanwhile, we sit twiddling our thumbs. There's nothing that bugs me more than somebody procrastinating."

Elder Keller sat back, amusement flickering in his eyes, his mouth quirked in fun. "Oh? Is that right? I remember someone saying he intended to start a diet next week. That was what, two months ago?" He glanced at Steve. "To my son, a diet is something he keeps putting off while he keeps putting on."

"Hey, no fair!" Tommy exclaimed. "I didn't say anything about a diet. That's one of those four-letter words we don't use around here. How did we get on that subject anyway?"

The old man cackled gleefully. "You were talking about procrastinating. Maybe you should put that telephone fellow and yourself both on your weekly departmental tag-in list. If it works for your directors, it's bound to work for you and him, too."

Steve delightedly watched the good-natured ribbing between father and son. Now he spoke up.

"What's a weekly tag-in?"

Elder Keller looked at Steve in surprise. "Boy, you don't miss anything, do you? I was just getting ready to

157

go into that. It's the last step in the four-part planning process. It's the key that makes the whole system work. If a pastor fails to follow through on this final point, the first three will eventually crumble and the management program will collapse."

Steve frowned. "A weekly meeting? I thought all this was supposed to save time!"

"It does. The entire tag-in takes less than five minutes."

"When do you do it?"

"On your regular Bible study night."

"What's the tag-in for?"

"Several reasons, but mostly to overcome procrastination."

The elderly preacher helped himself to the coffee and handed a cup to Steve. Tommy perched himself on the edge of the sofa arm to listen.

"You see, Steve, the major problem you discover with volunteer directors is their tendency to put responsibilities off until the last minute. This is a common problem that most pastors find. It is estimated that only about five percent of people in our society are self-motivated. The other ninety-five percent need prodding and encouragement. The tag-in does just that. It also improves the quality of work performed. Jobs that are done in a rush at the last minute are usually done poorly."

"Hmm . . . okay, how does it work?" Steve still looked rather doubtful.

"Simple. On your Bible study night, always make a habit of dismissing with prayer. Even if you give an altar call that night, still say a closing prayer. Then, just before you pray, ask all your department heads to come to the front. After they are grouped on the side, then dismiss the service."

Steve cocked an eyebrow in puzzlement. "Why before?"

"Because if I ask to see all of them at the front immediately *following* dismissal, it takes some of them ten minutes to finally make it up there."

Steve grinned. "You have that right."

The elderly pastor continued. "Following prayer, you walk directly down from the pulpit to tag in with them. Your secretary should come up with the directors and bring the tag-in list from the last monthly council. The tag-in list is made up of anything they need to do that month from their one-year plans, plus any directives or assignments that you gave them. You may have asked a director to follow through on two or three jobs. Now, you simply ask how the assignment is going.

"I might ask my Sunday school superintendent, 'Did you order that literature yet? You have? Okay, check that off. How about that substitute position—did you talk to Sister Smith about it? Oh, you're going to do that tonight? All right, now about that banquet facility . . . oh, you're going to do that next week? Fine. Okay, you're dismissed.' You might spend ten to fifteen seconds tagging in with the first director, then go on to the next. In three or four minutes, you're through. You've tagged in with each director. You know the status of everything that needed to be done."

Steve nodded slowly. "But what if a problem comes up, or the director must explain something that will take longer than fifteen seconds?"

"If that be the case, ask that director to remain until

159

you've tagged in with the others, then come back to him. That way you don't make the other directors wait."

"And if they haven't completed their assignments?"

"Oh, don't worry too much about that. They won't procrastinate long. A director might tell you at the first tag-in that he didn't get around to something. He might even tell you the same at the second and perhaps even the third. However, I can almost guarantee that the job will be done by the fourth. It's just too uncomfortable to keep coming back, week after week, and report in front of all the other directors that he hasn't done anything yet. The whole key to effective delegation can be summed up in this one statement: *People don't do what you expect; they do what you inspect!*"

"That makes sense!" Steve said with a grin. "So the weekly tag-in is just a quick, five-minute inspection."

"Right. And you never need to get angry or upset with anyone for not doing his job, because you always work at least three months in advance. This allows you considerable time to be flexible before anything becomes critical. Yet the best part is how little time it takes. Five minutes and you should never think about it again for the rest of the week. And that's another benefit of the tag-in: it keeps you from worrying. You know exactly where everything stands in every department.

"You see, Steve, that is true of the entire four-part planning process. It's designed from beginning to end to free the pastor from the time-robbing task of involved administration. The retreat and one-year plan are only once a year. The monthly council requires only a few hours a month. The tag-in is only five minutes a week. That adds up to maybe two and a half hours per month. So a pastor can push aside all the minor details and devote himself to doing what God called Him to do: pastor."

"But Elder, what if I end up with a director who is just plain lazy? What if he can't be depended upon? Do I just kick him out? How can I do that without making him feel bad or lose face before the church?"

Up to that moment, Tommy Keller had sat quietly and listened. Now he spoke.

"You know, Steve, I had somewhat that same situation when I took the church from my father. Our head usher was an elderly fellow and was totally devoted to Dad's ministry. When Dad retired, this fellow lost interest in ushering altogether. I couldn't get him to follow through on anything. Yet rather than embarrass the man by asking him to step down, I just carried on business as usual. After about four months he came to me and asked if he could be relieved of his position."

"Why?"

"Because with this kind of management process it's too uncomfortable to do nothing. Look, Steve, if you will conduct an annual retreat, require each director to hand in a one-year plan, start scheduling monthly councils, collect reports, and hold a weekly tag-in, you will never need to dismiss an incompetent director. They will ask or beg to be dismissed. When there's that much heat in the kitchen, if you don't want to work, you get out. It's just downright embarrassing to sit there and report every month that you did nothing!"

"Whoo-ee!" Steve exclaimed. "I can see what you mean. It becomes almost a peer-pressure situation."

"Now you've got it," Elder Keller said. "And nobody likes to look bad in front of his peers. So after using the system for a year or so, you'll end up with a group of leaders who are faithful, hard working, and committed to the work of God.''

Steve sat back in his chair, his mind in a whirl as he pictured his little church working under such a system. "Wouldn't it be great," he murmured, "not to worry about all the minor details of making the church operate. How much more I could accomplish if everyone would do his job!"

He shook his head again. "If only I had known this two years ago. I can see now why I've been stuck in one spot for so long. When I tried to delegate, my leaders struggled because of my rotten management. Rather than chew someone out, I would do the work myself. As it stands now, I'm doing almost everything myself. We can't grow larger because I can't handle anything larger. It's like a vicious circle. The larger we grow, the more I would have to do . . . no wonder pastors have nervous breakdowns.''

Elder Keller sat back with a sigh. "Several years ago I realized that God called me to be a pastor, not a corporate executive officer. When I spent all my time in administration, my church's spiritual growth suffered. Finally, in desperation, I prayed for guidance on how to keep all the church ministries and departments functioning and still devote most of my time to spiritual matters. The four-part planning system is what the Lord showed me. If something struggles for survival with this kind of a framework, then I'm better off letting it die. My time and spiritual health are too important to sacrifice on dead or dying programs.''

Steve made a few more notations in his notebook

before closing it. "Elder, I can't tell you how much you've helped me today. For the first time in months, I can see a glimmer of hope. It's going to work; I just know it. But I need to call it quits for now. My brain has reached overload, and if I try to absorb any more, I'll blow a fuse."

Tommy stood to his feet and stretched. "I hoped you would say that. Dad's a regular slave driver when it comes to this kind of stuff. I've told him to slow down, but he keeps saying he must teach fifty young men, and you're only number thirty-six."

"Thirty-seven," Elder Keller corrected. "And every one of them who's using it has a growing church. You will too, Steve, because it's always the Lord's will to grow."

Tommy reached and slapped Steve on the back. "Been good meeting you, Steve. By the way, if you're free tonight, I would like you to speak to our young men. Every Tuesday evening I teach young men's leadership training here at the church. We would be honored if you would bring us something."

"I . . . I don't know," Steve stammered. "What would I say?"

"Just whatever's on your heart. Anything concerning Christian service and working for God. It's at 7:30. We'll be looking forward to it."

And with that he walked out, leaving Steve groping for an excuse.

Elder Keller chuckled. "No use trying to back out. Besides, it's a real honor: that leadership training class is his pride and joy. Tommy places a strong emphasis on Christian service and development."

"How's that?" Steve asked, his interest sparked

again.

"Later!" Elder Keller exclaimed. "I'm ready for my afternoon nap. We'll talk about the importance of leadership development another time."

With a wave of his hand, he ushered Steve out the door.

Chapter Seven

Developing Leaders

The next morning Steve awoke with a start, a loud metallic clanging abruptly interrupting his shallow slumber. The dizzy fogginess of sleep caused a moment's confusion. He shook his head to bring himself fully awake. Several more seconds passed before he could determine that the imposing noise came from outside.

He slipped out of bed and peered through the louvered shades to the large back yard below.

Standing by the back door, Elder Keller banged Lazarus's food pan against the tree stump a couple times more, dislodging the last few scraps from the last night's dinner. Setting it down before his gray-muzzled friend, he spooned the dog's breakfast out of the can. The floppy-eared hound wasted no time in getting down to business.

Steve yawned and stretched, allowing his gaze to lift toward the line of trees that encompassed the grounds. Thin, feathery wisps of fog curled about the dense shrubs and thickets. The grass sparkled with silvery dew, reflecting a morning sun that was now well up in the cloudless, azure sky. Somewhere close a robin sounded its melodious song and was answered by another farther away in the trees. With a deep contented sigh Steve glanced at his watch. It was time to get up.

A half hour later, showered, shaved, and dressed, he sat mothering a hot cup of coffee. His elderly host stood in front of the stove grilling flapjacks in a huge, black, cast-iron skillet.

"I have to go to Woodville today," Brother Keller said, glancing over his shoulder at Steve, "and buy a new housing for the main well pump. The old one is cracked and making such a racket it's driving me and the neighbors berserk. Brother Tullison, the church maintenance director, said he would replace it if I would pick up a new one."

He set the pile of golden-brown buckwheat cakes on the table and poured some coffee for himself. "You're welcome to go with me if you wish. Or, if you'd rather stay and relax, I'll be back around noon and we'll go to the church. You were up late last night after the leadership training class. You must be tired."

"Truthfully, I feel great," Steve replied. He poured thick maple syrup over his steaming stack and added another generous slab of fresh butter. "Tommy began showing me the new curriculum he's using for his class, and we both lost track of time. His whole concept of leadership development is tremendous. I just wish my church was large enough to merit classes like that."

Elder Keller paused, his fork frozen halfway to his mouth and one craggy, gray eyebrow arched in surprise. Watching his reaction, Steve had the distinct impression he had said something wrong.

"Well, you know what I mean . . . " The young man

fumbled uncomfortably to defend his statement. "I don't really have enough young men to hold a class like that, and . . . well, some couldn't come anyway because they work nights."

"Hmm. . . ," the elderly pastor replied as he continued eating. He took a careful swallow of the steaming hot coffee and then cleared his throat loudly. "I wasn't aware that a church had to be a certain size or meet certain conditions to begin developing responsible leadership. Nothing in the Bible says that. To the contrary, Jesus only had twelve faithful followers, yet he trained them. And who said they all have to be young? And for that matter, who says they all have to be men? The best visitor-follow-up director I ever had was a woman in her fifties."

"But how would I pick and choose?" Steve argued. "I can't very well show favoritism for some to the exclusion of others. In a small church I'd be asking for trouble."

"The first criterion for leadership, young man, is a desire to lead. What I would do is go privately to those whom you think have real potential. Let them know that you feel God wants to use them in some way and you would like them to attend the training sessions. Then open it up for all who wish to come. If half the church shows up, so much the better. The material should be such that anyone who attends would benefit. Teach and train those who come as if every one of them will some day be a department head. Only let me warn you: those who you thought had no potential might surprise you."

"And if my potential leader doesn't come?"

"Then he is not leadership material. Remember this, Steve: if an individual can't be faithful to a weekly or biweekly class, then most likely he will never be faithful

167

to an assigned position. Jesus said, 'Thou hast been faithful over a few things, I will make thee ruler over many.' Always start your prospective leaders out slowly. As they prove themselves dependable with minor tasks, then you can promote them to greater responsibility. Help them grow and mature into a leadership position step by step."

Steve nodded thoughtfully, his eyes reflecting a faraway look. "So I guess leadership development is important—even in a church the size of mine."

"It's important, son, in any church—that is, if you are planning to grow. One great void in our movement is a lack of trained saints to help the ministry in leadership. Our churches are only now becoming aware of this need. Everywhere you look you see the signs of stress and burnout in the ministry. One man can carry a church by himself only so long. Preachers are waking up to the fact that they can't sail a large ship alone. The bigger the ship, the more help is needed.

"Your growth, Steve, is directly tied to your leadership resources. As I said, once you reach around seventy, you must delegate responsibility or become stagnant. If you don't have reliable, trained individuals to help carry the load, your progress will stop until you can develop them—a stop that often destroys your momentum. If you want a church of three hundred five years from now, you must begin training the leaders needed to operate a church of that size today. An ingredient I have found in all large, growing churches is this: the pastor is dedicated to developing effective Christian leadership before he actually needs it."

Steve sat quietly eating, letting the elder pastor's

words sink in. Then after a pause, he asked, "What about the few department heads I currently have. Would I put them in this class, too?"

The old pastor nodded. "For a while, yes. And if they are quality leadership material, they will want to attend because they will want to be as effective a leader as possible. Psychologists tell us that a powerful desire in all people is the desire to succeed. No one wants to be a failure. This is especially true of your department heads. They want to work for God, or they wouldn't have accepted the position. They would simply forget the headache of leadership and spend evenings and Saturdays at their leisure.

"No, Steve, your department heads accepted the burden of responsibility because they desired to further the cause of Christ. Now it's your responsibility as pastor to help them be their best." As he spoke he stabbed a long, bony finger in the young man's direction. "Let me say it again: successful leaders are not born, they are developed. That's why the most important hour you spend each week is the one you invest in your prospective leaders."

Key Concept Eight

Thou shalt impart wisdom and knowledge to thy people that they may grow and prosper in their calling.

The young man nodded his agreement. He leaned forward, his voice alive with excitement. "What do you suggest I use as a curriculum?"

"That choice will be yours. You want your leaders to have basic people skills. I started with Dale Carnegie's *How To Win Friends and Influence People.* Not only is it a classic on human relations, it's also excellent for soul winning instruction, because you must win a friend before you can win a soul. I bought them each a paperback, and we studied one chapter a week. However, other books are effective also. I have a list of books and tapes at the church that I'll give you.[1] Many are motivational books that you'll find in the self-improvement section of any bookstore. But when you teach them, you must be careful to give the proper Bible basis and remove any humanistic slant.

"I also taught a lot of soul-winning and church-growth concepts. I did one eight-part series on various denominations and how they err from Scripture. I did another on how to teach a home Bible study. I usually had a three- or four-week break between each series. Then, each time I started a new subject, I'd announce it to the church for all who wished to attend."

"Boy," Steve exclaimed, "that sounds great, except for one thing: when did you find time to study all those books?"

The elderly pastor snorted. "I never did *find* time. I had to *take* time. You see, although this material was excellent for them, it proved to be even more important for me. A pastor's like a log burning in Grandma's cookstove. After a while a layer of ash will build up and choke out the flame. Then the fire begins to die. What the log needs is a hefty poke—something to knock the ashes off.

By making my directors study, it forced me to study also, and it kept us both from falling into a mental rut."

"How was your attendance?"

"Some subjects were better attended than others, but overall it was excellent. It was well known in my church that my leaders and workers were chosen from those who attended leadership training. And rightly so, for I strongly believe that all who are truly living for God will have not only a desire to work for God but also a desire to be the best they can be. It's a natural yearning.

"You see, Steve, Jesus first told Peter, 'Feed my lambs.' The lambs are your new converts and the young children in your church. They have their own special diet. They can't be placed into leadership too soon or it will hurt them, although you can begin to nurture them in that direction. Jesus then said, 'Feed my sheep.' This is your average saint. All will not be leaders, but all are called to be laborers. Everyone has his or her place in the Lord's body.

"The Lord's third commandment appears to be simply a repeat of His previous one. However, it may have a further connotation, for one ancient translation renders it 'Feed my *rams.'* Your rams are your leaders, your Bible study teachers, your best soul winners. They are the natural leaders within the flock of God. They need special diets because they burn a lot of spiritual calories. When rams are not fed properly, they'll bust through the fence looking for food. It is my conviction that many so-called problem saints are simply leaders without direction."

Steve nodded his head again, sipping his coffee slowly. "Makes sense. I have a few people in my church who would fit in that category. If I don't keep them busy doing something constructive, they usually find something to do on their own. Unfortunately, it's often more hurtful than helpful." He set his coffee down. "All right, when do you suggest I teach this class?"

"I taught mine on Friday evening before youth service," Elder Keller replied. "We started at 6:30 and I taught for exactly forty-five minutes. We finished with ten to fifteen minutes of prayer. Most would then go to youth service. Some left to teach Bible studies or do follow-up visitation."

"Why did Tommy change it to Tuesday night?" Steve questioned.

"Some people couldn't make it by 6:30 on Friday because of work, so he moved it to 7:30 on Tuesday. However, he's planning to change it back."

"Why?"

"Because it ties up another night of the week. You must be careful, son, not to plan much activity on off-church nights. I can't stress this strongly enough. It keeps people from becoming involved in outreach and home Bible studies. Your people also need family time.

"For example," Brother Keller continued, "if an individual teaches a home Bible study on Monday evening, has leadership class on Tuesday evening, church service on Wednesday, does follow-up visitation on Thursday, youth service on Friday . . . get the picture? Before long, he'll either burn out or his wife will leave him."

"Boy, I've been there," Steve laughed, "and the hurrier I go, the behinder I get."

The old man smiled. "Exactly. So schedule your teaching sessions around regular service times and leave off nights open for them to apply what they've learned."

Elder Keller stood up with a yawn and stretched. He glanced toward the back door, for Lazarus was scratching to be let in. "If you'll help me do these dishes, I think we can be back in time for you to rest before preaching tonight."

"What?" Steve exclaimed. "I'm not preaching tonight!"

"Oh, I forgot to tell you," Brother Keller said with a sympathetic grin. "Tommy called earlier and asked me to tell you to be ready. He said that lesson you taught last night on commitment was so good, he wants the whole church to hear it."

"Then tell him to play the tape," Steve mumbled nervously. "I've never preached to that many people before."

"Terrific. It's time to get used to it. When you start growing, you'll probably have twice that number." And with that, the aged pastor began to clear the dishes.

Appearances Can Deceive

Twenty minutes later found them traveling in Brother Keller's dilapidated yellow '64 Ford pickup towards Woodville. Trees and thick, green undergrowth crowded close to the narrow country highway, winding past farms and an occasional orchard. The sun had burned off the ground fog and evaporated the morning dew, yet still left an edge of crispness in the November air.

Steve had been quietly lost in thought ever since they had left the house. He gazed out the side window, unmindful of the picturesque countryside spread before them.

"What's on your mind, son?" Brother Keller asked.

"Oh," the young pastor replied wistfully, "I was thinking about starting a leadership class as you sug-

173

gested. I've been going over the church in my mind trying to pick out my potential leaders." Steve shook his head
and shrugged with resignation. "My problem, Elder, is
that my people are mostly simple country folk. I'm not
blessed with many natural leaders like you. I guess some
churches have it and others don't."

Elder Keller's eyebrows shot up. "Oh?" He replied
with a sarcastic tone. "My, my, my . . . you poor mistreat-
ed lad. God just hasn't been fair to you, has He? The Lord
probably figured—"

Steve waved his hand to interrupt, turning around
to face him. "I don't mean it that way. I know I sound
as though I'm feeling sorry for myself, Elder, but facts
are facts. You can't turn a mule into a racehorse. I just
don't have any real leader-type people."

Brother Keller held the wheel with one hand and
reached into his pocket to pull out his wallet with the
other. Glancing down, he thumbed through it until he
found a worn, tattered card. Without a word, he handed
it to Steve. It said:

Everyone
Is a Potential Winner
•
Some People
Are Disguised
as Losers.
•
Don't Let
Their Appearance
Fool You.

As Steve started to reply the older man cut him off. "I know what you're going to say before you say it, son. So, before you try arguing with me, let me tell you about some research that was done a few years back. Ever heard of Dr. Robert Rosenthal?"

The young man shook his head.

"He's a leading researcher in what they call behavioral science. Real smart fellow. He directed over three hundred experiments at Harvard University in human expectations. They had an article on him a while back in *Time* magazine—a fascinating piece of research. One particular experiment sticks in my memory.[2] It started at the beginning of a regular school year.

"He called in three elementary teachers and told them that they had been selected above all other teachers in the city because of their superior teaching ability—that observation and testing had showed no teacher tallied better. So they were being asked to participate in a study using high I.Q. children. The ninety brightest students in the school district were to be given to them for one year, thirty pupils in each class.

"The study," Elder Keller continued, "was supposed to measure academic growth when superior, high-aptitude children were coupled with superior, high-quality teachers. However, the study required that two strict conditions be maintained: neither the children nor the children's parents were ever to know that an experiment was being performed. The three teachers eagerly agreed. To them, it was the chance of a lifetime.

"Well, to make a long story short, the students' progress was phenomenal. The three classes completed the year with the highest scores in the city—over a ninety

175

percent average in every subject."

Elder Keller paused and Steve glanced up. "So?"

"So," the old pastor continued, "the real purpose of the experiment was only then revealed. Get this: neither the three teachers nor the ninety students were of superior ability in any way. All had been chosen by computer completely at random. The only difference was what the teachers thought, in other words, what they expected of themselves and what they expected of their students."

Steve stared at Brother Keller, his mouth gaping open, dumfounded. Several times he started to say something, only to check himself. After several minutes he finally spoke, his voice but a whisper. "So what you are saying, sir, is that it's mainly my attitude that determines how many leaders I have." It wasn't a question, but a statement.

The older man nodded.

"And," Steve continued slowly, "if I think of my people as just a bunch of country hicks, that's all they'll ever be." The older man nodded again.

Steve again gazed out of the pickup window at the passing countryside. In his mind he saw his people. Country folk, yes, but sincere in their zeal to work for God. He saw the times he had taken out his frustration, condemning them as he had preached. He had even wondered within himself at times why God hadn't sent him something better to work with. He knew the Bible taught that the body of Christ was not deficient, not in any way anemic or feeble. The Lord's body wasn't missing an arm or a leg. It wasn't crippled or weak. God had empowered every church with what it needed to reach its city, but he had always thought his church must be an exception.

How wrong he had been!

Steve turned back around with a sigh, his thoughts still spinning. "You know, Elder, what you just said reminded me of something I read when I was a kid. It was a biography of Thomas Edison. I'm sure you've heard that as a boy Edison did poor in school, so poor that his teacher sent him home with a note saying he was incapable of learning—retarded. His mother refused to accept that, so she taught him herself. The rest is history.

"In a sense," Steve continued, his voice shaking, "I've done the same thing as that teacher. In my mind I've sent my directors home without giving them a fair chance. Yet the fact is, I never had any real faith in them in the first place. Boy, I've sure blown it."

The old man returned a kind smile. "Don't be too hard on yourself, son. I heard a story of a fellow who messed up worse than that. It seems that one spring, some time before the Civil War, a boy in search of work went to the farm of a fellow named Worthy Taylor up in Ohio. The farmer knew nothing about the boy except that his name was Jim. He needed help so he gave the boy a job.

"Jim spent the summer cutting stove wood and doing various other chores. He ate in the kitchen and slept in the hayloft. Before the summer was over, Jim had fallen in love with Worthy Taylor's daughter. When the farmer heard of it, he refused to let them marry. He told his daughter bluntly that the young man had no money, no name, and no potential.

In his shame, Jim put his belongings in his battered carpetbag and disappeared. Thirty-five years passed before Farmer Taylor tore down his old barn to build a new one. On a rafter above the hayloft, he discovered that

Jim had carved his full name—JAMES A. GARFIELD. He was then president of the United States."

Steve grinned broadly. "Guess that taught him not to be so quick to judge!"

"But how about you, son? I wonder how many potential leaders God has in your church that are out tending sheep or hidden among the stuff? How many Davids or Sauls do you have waiting for a man of God to call them?"

Steve fell silent again as the old pickup bounced noisily across the railroad tracks and entered the city limits.

Pump Housings or Watch Springs?

Woodville reminded Steve of the old-time pictures he used to see of towns during the Depression. Small clapboard store buildings, somewhat grayed from the dusty street, stared with empty eyes across the narrow boulevard. A gas station with antique round-top pumps sat on one corner, and a faded Coca-Cola sign was painted on the building's side. Few cars or pedestrians were in sight. A couple of men in overalls sat on a bench in front of the country drugstore drinking pop and talking loudly, occasionally with a burst of laughter. Brother Keller pulled up in front of a concrete block building that was aptly named Wayne's Water Works and Pump Supply. Steve settled back to wait as the old pastor went inside.

It took only a few minutes for Brother Keller to pick up the part. As they drove out of town and back onto the highway, Elder Keller pointed with his thumb back to the new, shiny, red pump housing in the pickup bed behind them.

"How much do you think that cost?" he asked.

"Oh, you paid about fifty dollars, didn't you?" Steve

178

replied.

"Yep. Not much for twenty pounds of high-grade cast steel. Now, what if they used that same steel for machine nuts and bolts instead of a pump part? It probably would have tripled its value. Or had they made precision ball bearings, it would have brought several hundred dollars. Now, twenty pounds of top quality needles would be worth several thousand dollars. Fine watch springs would be hundreds of thousands—and all from the same hunk of metal. Why the difference, son?"

"The amount of time and effort to produce it, of course."

"Then remember this: the amount of time and effort you devote to training and developing your people will determine whether they are pump housings or watch springs. It's ironic that most churches spend sixty percent of their income on the building and less than one percent to train the people—when it's people that bring growth."

"I never thought of that," the young man admitted. "If it's people that bring growth, it certainly would make sense to invest in people."

"Well said. And when you say invest, realize that's exactly what it takes. If you are reluctant to spend money on your directors, then don't bother appointing them."

"You mean I should pay them?"

"No, that's not what I mean, at least not in the literal sense. Many pastors think that if they could only hire a full-time assistant, then everything would operate properly. That's not true. The most important traits needed from your leadership can't be purchased.

"You see, son, you can't buy a man's time. Oh, you

can buy his physical presence at a given place. You can even buy a measured number of physical motions per hour. But you can't buy his enthusiasm, his loyalty, or his devotion of heart, mind, and soul. These are qualities that cannot be purchased. If a man gives these to you, it's because you've earned them.

"It's the law of sowing and reaping, son. What you get will be exactly what you give. If you are ever going to develop quality leadership, you are going to have to give of your time, your concern, your efforts, and, yes, your money. Department directors have definite needs. If you don't fulfill those needs, they'll look somewhere else."

"What do you mean by needs?"

"By needs, I mean the basic desires that all people have. Here, let me show you." Elder Keller reached under the seat and withdrew a clipboard. "Hand me some of that scrap paper down by your feet. That's it; clip it in so I can draw something."

"Hadn't you better let me drive?" Steve asked with a startled glance. The pickup had swerved over the center line.

"Naw! I could drive this road with my eyes closed. Now, hand me your pen." Glancing away from the road for a few seconds, he quickly drew the following:[3]

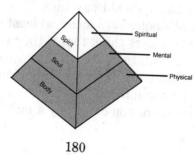

"You know, Steve, that man is by nature body, soul, and spirit—or physical, mental, and spiritual. He has basic needs in each of these areas. It doesn't matter if he's a saint or a sinner; in this respect all people are the same.

"Now, the business world satisfies a man's physical need with money. Money forms the foundation of its motivational methods and is the major reward for a job well done. Next, a person's mental or intellectual need is fulfilled by being constantly challenged with job advancement, improved skills, and training. Finally, his spiritual need is addressed by understanding his job purpose. An individual must feel that his job is important and needed; he must have a sense of pride and self-worth in both the company and in his position. If any employer fails to fulfill these three basic needs in an employee, then he runs the risk of losing him. Or if he does stay, his heart won't be in it.

"Now the church must do the same if its leadership is to be dedicated and devoted. Only we must change it around a bit. We should put the major emphasis on the spiritual instead of the physical. It's more like this."

Glancing down a second time, Brother Keller quickly sketched the following:

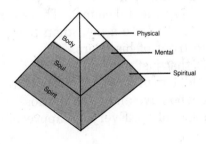

"The very foundation of our Christian service is our tremendous sense of purpose. This appeals to our spiritual nature. From the janitor to the song leader, everyone needs to feel that his position is important, appreciated, and essential to the work of God. You see, *know-how* only becomes important when you know *why*. Know-how lets you drive it; know-why will drive you. All the knowledge and information in the world is useless unless something motivates you to apply it. Only realize, Steve, that your leaders will not know how or why unless you tell them."

"So what you are saying," Steve injected, "is that all people need to be rewarded for their labors. Understanding their job's importance and purpose can be their reward in the spiritual area."

"Yes, but more than just purpose and worth—also some physical expression of appreciation."

"How do I do that," Steve queried, "if I don't pay them?"

"Oh, any number of ways: certificates and plaques of achievement, letters of appreciation, thank-you's in the church bulletin, awards and honors at the yearly leadership appreciation banquet (which, by the way, should be an annual event in any church). Yet, most important is expressing your appreciation to your directors at the monthly departmental council. There is no greater compliment you can give a man than to be recognized and praised in front of his peers."

"Isn't that just a carnal ego trip?" Steve wondered.

The older man laughed. "There are only two kinds of people who have an ego, son: those who admit it and then the rest of us. Everyone appreciates being appreciated."

"I guess you're right," Steve admitted. "Nobody likes a selfish, self-centered snob for a pastor."

"No, young man, they don't. And if a pastor only takes from his directors and never gives, his ministry will die in the same manner as the Dead Sea. The Bible instructs us to give honor to whom honor is due."

"Sounds good. And I guess my directors' intellectual needs are covered through leadership instruction?"

"Exactly. The material you use should continually challenge them to improve their skills and abilities for the work of God."

"Fine, yet there's something I don't understand, Elder. These leadership development classes you said are taught once a week for forty-five minutes. Yet the other day you mentioned having leadership training during the first half-hour of each monthly department council. What's the difference?"

"The weekly class, Steve, is open to all who desire to be used in a leadership capacity or further their skills in the work of God. The material you teach should have a broad application and be highly motivational. However, the subjects you teach to your department heads at the monthly council should be specific to the area of managing and directing people. These are the skills they will need if their departments are going to grow."

"What subjects, for example?"

"Subjects such as how to motivate people, how to develop a team spirit, how to get people to think with and act favorably toward you, how to organize, how to manage your time, and so on. At the weekly class, I liked to use a good paperback to teach from. However, at the monthly council, I'd normally give them a cassette tape. After they listened to it on their own time, I taught the same topic, giving it the proper biblical perspective. I don't know if that's the best way, but it worked well for me."[4]

"Sounds as though it would do the job. But don't all those books and tapes get expensive after a while?"

"Sure. They add up to several hundred dollars each year. That's what I meant by investment. Compliments and kind words are important, but unless they are accompanied by kind deeds, they begin to sound hollow. I made it a point to spend a little money on my department directors. I always tried to pay for the annual planning retreat. I also hosted the annual leaders appreciation banquet. I always remembered their birthdays and anniversaries and gave them a small gift at Christmas.

"I would also cover expenses so they could go to training seminars: youth director to the youth convention, outreach director to the council on church growth, Sunday school director to the Sunday school convention, and so on. Occasionally, I'd take a director and his or her spouse out to dinner. I've found out, Steve, that if you reward performance, you get performers. If you reward with peanuts, all you get is monkeys."

"So what you're saying is, do unto your directors as you would have them do unto you," Steve said, flashing a smile.

"Now you've got it. If I want trust, I must trust them. If I want them to listen to me, I must be willing to listen to them. And most important, if I want them to be patient with me when I make mistakes, I must do the same with them. The only person who never makes a mistake is the fellow who does nothing. Since I want my directors to do something, I must be willing to let them slip-up occasionally. When they blow it, they at least show they were trying.

"I know several pastors, Steve, who refused to delegate because nobody could do it exactly as they wanted it done. I had one man even tell me it was easier to do everything himself than it was to fix the messes his directors made. That pastor will never grow. By his very actions he undermines his directors' faith in themselves. A poor pastor inspires people to have confidence only in him. A good pastor inspires people to have confidence not only in him but also in themselves and in God."

The young man gazed at the elderly man who sat in the driver's seat beside him, marvelling within himself at the wisdom he had just heard. He knew this drive down a winding country highway would long be remembered.

"Thank you, Brother Keller," Steve said, his voice quiet yet deeply sincere. "You don't know how much I appreciate what you've said today. To think I might have gone home and waited until God sent me what I called leadership material, when all along they sat in the pews in front of me waiting to be developed."

Steve slowly leaned back and closed his eyes as if he were suddenly exhausted. Then, opening his eyes once again, he murmured almost to himself, "Maybe . . . maybe I can get Brother Marker, my Sunday school superintendent, to give me another chance . . ." Steve trailed off and closed his eyes again. He was silent for the rest of the ride home.

Chapter Eight

A Prayer-Conditioned Church

That evening when Steve arrived at the church, he was surprised to see the long parking lot already beginning to fill. He glanced at his watch: quarter to seven. He had purposely come early, leaving while Elder Keller was still getting ready, so that he might have time to pray before service. Yet there were at least fifty cars in the spaces around the church. I hope my watch hasn't stopped, he thought.

After parking in the space reserved for visiting ministers, he walked hurriedly to the main entrance. As he approached, he was greeted by an older gentleman, apparently a doorkeeper, who smiled in a friendly way, shook his hand, and opened the door. He stepped into the vestibule and was immediately met by an attractive young woman wearing a flower corsage and a brass pin labeled "HOSTESS."

"Praise the Lord," she said with a pleasant smile. "It is so good to have you with us this evening. Is this your first time to visit?''

"Uh . . . yes it is . . . at least for a church service,'' Steve answered with a faint grin. He could tell she didn't know who he was. But his hesitation somehow tipped her off, because a flash of recognition crossed her face.

"Are you Pastor Martin?''

"Guilty as charged.''

She laughed brightly. "Then there is no need for you to fill out a guest card. Pastor Keller mentioned that you would be speaking this evening and to watch for you. I believe he said he would be in his office.''

Steve thanked her and entered the double doors of the sanctuary. Inside a few people were scattered around in small groups. The sound of intercession floated from the prayer room behind the platform, filling the auditorium with a holy presence. From the volume of the voices, he guessed that a sizable number must be praying. He shook his head in confusion. Why were so many people here so early?

Pastor Tommy Keller stepped out of his office to meet him as Steve walked down the center aisle. The hostess had buzzed him that Pastor Martin had arrived.

"Praise the Lord, my friend,'' Tommy called.

"Did I get my time mixed up?'' Steve asked as he shook his hand. "Does church start at 7:00 or 7:30?''

"At 7:30,'' Tommy replied. "You're early yet. Church doesn't start for another forty-five minutes.''

"I was just wondering. There were so many cars in the parking lot. You have something special going on?''

"No, we just have a lot of people who come early to pray. The majority can't come this early because of work, so they'll be here around 7:00. But those who can will often arrive an hour before service. The Intercessors are a strong ministry in our church."

"The Intercessors? What's that?"

"That's what we call our prayer-team ministry. At Apostolic Tabernacle, our Prayer and Missions Ministry is a department by itself. Sister Perry oversees this department and helps me organize and promote it. She's one of those classic, old-time prayer warriors."

"What do they do—I mean, besides pray?"

"Come on and I'll show you."

This Church Is Prayer Conditioned

Tommy led the way through the arched doorway to the right of the platform into the long, curved prayer room. The lights were dimmed to a pale glow, but Steve could still make out the row of padded altars that lined the walls. Several rows of chairs, back to back, were also spaced at intervals down the center. The shadowy forms of people kneeling, walking, and some even lying prostrate on the floor in earnest supplication were faintly visible. The sound of their weeping and worship rose and fell in a swelling tide. The presence of the Holy Ghost filled the room strongly, sending chill bumps down Steve's neck.

They watched for a moment before Tommy led the way back into the sanctuary.

"As you could see," Tommy continued, "most of those praying are elderly, although not all. An hour before each service, Sister Perry meets with those who are able. She'll bring a word of encouragement and take prayer requests; then they will pray until service time. The prayer room is packed by 7:10. Most of our people try to come for at least a half hour of prayer.

189

"Boy," Steve exclaimed, his voice full of admiration, "that's tremendous! But how do you get them to come so early? Getting my people to preservice prayer is like trying to get my kid to eat turnips. I practically have to get on my hands and knees and beg."

"Well, we didn't get this way overnight. It took a lot of work, in fact, years of praying and teaching. However, I also require anyone who is in leadership—department heads, Sunday school teachers, choir members, Bible study teachers, and so on—to set an example by praying at least a half hour before service. It's part of the requirements in their job descriptions. If they come late, I encourage them to go to the prayer room anyway. Most make it on time because they don't want to miss any of the worship service."

Steve's eyebrows arched in surprise. "I'm afraid if I did that I'd either lose my leadership or lose my worship service. With some of my people, I feel good if I can just get them there to start on time."

Tommy smiled and nodded his head understandingly. "I have some people like that too, but I refuse to let them discourage our prayer ministry. Sister Perry not only oversees the preservice prayer, but she also helps me organize our quarterly chain of prayer and fasting. We do this at the first of each quarter and go around the clock for several days.

"She also helps promote our annual prayer revival, schedules prayer partners for the new converts and home Bible study teachers, types and hands out a monthly prayer list, maintains the prayer request board in the prayer room, manages our prayer hot line, coordinates the prayer library of books and tapes, and so on.[1] Oh, and

190

I didn't mention our prayer checks."

"Prayer checks?"

"Sure. A prayer check is like a normal check, except instead of *cash* on demand, it will supply *prayer* on demand. The people to whom we give one can cash it in for whatever need they have. If the check is for ten hours of prayer, then we will guarantee that amount of prayer for that need. We give them to missionaries, home missions pastors, and selected visitors. The prayer check is given with a self-stamped, self-addressed envelope, and they can mail it in whenever they wish. We received one the other day that I gave to a missionary three years ago."

"Hey, I like that. So when a sinner sends one in, you know they are in a good position for salvation."

"You catch on quickly. Prayer plays a major role in the growth of Apostolic Tabernacle." Tommy put his hand on Steve's shoulder as he led him back to the office. "And it sure makes a difference in our services. I think you'll see that tonight. This church is not only air conditioned, it's also prayer conditioned."

Steve listened to the increasing volume of praise and intercession coming from the prayer room behind them. "I'm sure it is," he said softly, more to himself than to the gentleman beside him. "I'm sure it is."

The service that evening was even more powerful and moving than Steve expected. The intense excitement was a tangible force as the power of God swept in mightily during the song service. In spite of four years of evangelizing, Steve had never felt anything like it. It wasn't pumped up or forced, but spontaneous and joyous. Twice the Spirit moved so that many shouted and danced with the thrill of worship. Steve grinned as he saw the surprised expression on the face of several visitors. However, the enthusiasm was obviously contagious, for several were raising their hands in praise and worship also.

Yet what gripped Steve most was the congregation's excitement over the Word of God. From the moment he stepped to the pulpit, the congregation began to back him up with shouts of hallelujah and glory. Never had preaching been so exciting or such a pleasure. They stood, they shouted, they clapped, they worshiped—it was pure joy! The invitation filled the altars, and a mother and her young daughter received the Holy Ghost. Another young man was baptized. The inspiration of what Steve saw and felt overwhelmed him.

Several times while working and praying in the altar, Steve paused and looked around him in amazement. It looked as if half the church was around the altars praying with someone. Those who weren't at the altar were praying at their seat. It was then he determined to bring this kind of spirit and excitement to his church. He would discover the secret or die trying.

Worship Is the Key

Later, after church was completely over, Steve sat at the kitchen table in Tommy's home. The house was located about six miles farther down the same road that Tommy's father lived on. Like Elder Keller's, the house stood well off the main road. Yet unlike his, it was practically new. It was a single-story ranch-style home with a cedar-shake roof. The decor revealed Sister Sandra Keller's appreciation of a country atmosphere. Everywhere Steve looked he saw something rustic, antique, or patchwork.

"I'm sorry your father-in-law wasn't feeling well tonight," he commented as Sister Sandra Keller filled his glass with iced tea. Elder Keller had left immediately following service, explaining that he was feeling bad.

"He's not sick as much as weak," she replied. "He's been having dizzy spells here of late, but he refuses to go to the doctor." She smiled sadly, "He's so stubborn about things like that."

Tommy came in just then and sat across from Steve. "My," he exclaimed, "you surely did preach tonight, my friend. That was tremendous. The lady who received the Holy Ghost tonight—it was only her second visit to our church."

"Anybody with half a mind could preach in an atmosphere like that, Pastor. Are all your services like that?"

"Not all the time. The Lord will often move in different ways. But most of the time, yes. The Spirit of the Lord brings liberty, and my people are certainly not inhibited by any means."

Steve gazed into his glass and slowly stirred his ice tea. "I'll occasionally have a real stem-winder, too. Not to tonight's extent, but a real good service. However, it's usually during a revival or something."

"Really?" Tommy said with surprise. "Dad always taught us that the only way a church could survive was to stay in revival. Around here revival is continuous."

"You mean one evangelist after another?" Now it was Steve's turn to be surprised.

Tommy laughed. "Not hardly. The people couldn't take it, and the church couldn't afford it. What I mean is that we try to maintain a continuous revival atmosphere."

"That can mean different things to different people. What do you mean by a revival atmosphere?"

"Well, for my church, a climate of revival means that folks are consistently receiving the Holy Ghost and being baptized. You'll find seekers in the altars, spontaneous and exuberant worship, and excited and happy people. They feel an attitude of faith and expectancy when they come to church, and a spirit of unity pervades the entire service. They are excited about the preaching and respond to the altar call. Also, miracles, healings, and spiritual gifts are evident."

"Well, sure!" Steve exclaimed, "If my services were like that all the time, I wouldn't need any church growth principles."

Tommy grinned. "Perhaps. I have often heard Dad say that you don't need any of his material to have revival. But if you're going to retain your growth and maximize the revival's effectiveness, you are going to have to have more than good services. His church growth principles are somewhat like the suspension system on a car: they allow you to go faster, carry more, and have a smoother ride."

Steve nodded his head. "I guess you're right. It takes more than shouting and running the aisles. But I'm sure your services help."

"They do more than help, Steve; they are essential. All the goals, programs, and plans in the world would be useless if, when people got there, the church was dead and dry. People have had enough of formalistic religion. They read in their Bibles that the New Testament church was alive and exciting. Miracles and conversions were the norm rather than the exception. People come to Pentecost expecting to find Pentecost. They want the church to be a happy place, a place where their souls are renewed and their hearts are mended. I read in a recent survey that, for eighty percent of Americans, true happiness is their number-one goal in life. So if my church is cold and lifeless, they'll look elsewhere.''

Key Concept Nine

Thou shalt call thy people continually unto prayer, preaching, and praise, for therewith shall many souls be born into the kingdom.

"OK," Steve responded, "how can I get the same kind of revival spirit in my church?"

Tommy shook his head. "I wish I could tell you in a simple one-two-three, step-by-step form. But the conditions that bring a revival atmosphere are not that easy to define. I asked Dad the same question when I first took my little church up north. He told me that if you tried to dismantle revival as you would an alarm clock, to see what makes it tick, you'd find that it has stopped ticking. Some say that continuous revival comes as the result of preaching. Others, that it comes out of worship. Still others, out of sowing seed. But truthfully, Steve, revival isn't that simple. I think it has many components. But I find that when I try to write it down as I would a recipe, then poof, it flies out the window. Why? Because I think revival is the very essence of God. And who can define God?"

"So what am I supposed to do?" Steve asked, his voice edged with frustration. "You say that a revival spirit is a critical key for growth, then you say you can't tell me how to get it. Now what?"

Tommy shrugged his shoulders. "Really, you're talking to the wrong person. Dad would give you a much better answer than I could. But I can possibly give you a few pointers. God helped me get that little church in Kentucky rolling before I came here. Even though much depends upon the individual church's characteristics as to what it needs, I've found that a few things are basic."

"Like what?"

"Like me, for instance," Tommy replied. "For the most part, saints are saints. But to a large degree, what gives a church its personality is the pastor. My church became a direct reflection of myself and my walk with God. If I was weak spiritually, they were weak spiritually. But if I was prayed up and full of victory, they were also. The old truism says, As the captain goes, so goes the ship."

"Boy, that's the truth," Steve said with a sigh. "I've been so discouraged these last few months, I've taken much of my frustration out on my church, and I can sure see the effect it's had on them."

Tommy nodded. "Solomon said, 'Without a vision the people perish.' The only vision your people will see is the one you show them. When your dream dies, so does theirs."

Steve stared at the table and shook his head sadly as he thought back over the last few months. It was easy to see that he had allowed the dream to fade. After a moment he glanced back up. "Okay, what else?"

"Well, as far as the services are concerned, I found

I have to have a real sensitivity to the Holy Ghost. A pastor *must* be in tune with God. During every service, my people are watching me and following my lead. I have to know what the Holy Ghost wants to do and move with Him. Not every service is made for shouting, nor is every service for weeping and repentance. If I'm not sensitive, the Holy Ghost will be grieved. Regardless of what type of service we have, the saints and the visitors should leave knowing that there has been a supernatural move of God."

Steve leaned back in his chair and studied the ceiling for a moment. Without looking back, he spoke. "Tell me, Brother—and if you'd rather not answer, just say so—how do you become sensitive to God that way? Don't get me wrong; I have felt God impress certain things upon me. But I'm never really positive of his direction. There's always that fog of doubt in the back of my mind as to whether I've heard him right or not."

"Steve, I don't know how it is with you, but with me, when I'm having trouble hearing from God, I know my flesh is standing in the way. And invariably the cause is that I'm not praying and fasting as I should. When I crucify the flesh and spend more time in prayer and the Word, I weaken the carnal man and strengthen the spiritual. The more I pray and fast, the more sensitive I become. It also builds my faith and destroys the fog of doubt that the devil tries to weaken me with."

Steve chewed softly on his lower lip. "Ouch, you hit me dead center again. Fasting isn't one of my strong points . . . and what you say makes sense. What else did you find that helped bring a revival spirit?"

"My, . . . so many things contributed. An emphasis on before-service prayer would have to be one. Also sowing a lot of seed. When people are seeking for God, and others are praying through regularly, it makes every service exciting. Nothing discourages a church quicker than empty altars."

"Or preachers," Steve injected.

"Right. Knowing that there will be visitors in almost any service really keeps me on my toes. I've got to make sure that I don't just preach a sermon, but that I have a message from the Lord. I keep a little sign on the pulpit facing me to remind myself of that. Did you see it?"

Steve thought for a moment, then smiled. "Okay, I remember. I wondered what that meant."

"It meant just what it said: AS IF IT WERE YOUR LAST. I can't allow myself to forget that this might be the last message I preach before the rapture, or perhaps the last that our visitors will ever hear."

"Keep going, Pastor," Steve said emphatically. "You're doing me a world of good. I can tell that you're a true preacher: you comfort the afflicted and afflict the comfortable."

Tommy grinned. "There's just one more thing, and I think it might be the most important."

"What's that?"

"Worship. Deep, heart-felt worship. Nothing will bring the power and presence of God like people who have their minds focused on Him."

Steve only nodded, so Tommy went on.

"I think worship is important to a revival atmosphere for five reasons, Steve." Tommy began counting them on his fingers.[2]

"First, David said the Lord inhabits the praises of Israel, so worship, in essence, invites the presence of God.

Second, it serves as a transition from the flesh into the Spirit. David said we should enter His gates with thanksgiving and into His courts with praise. Worship takes us into the very throne room of God. Third, it prepares the heart for the Word. Jesus said that the true worshipers would worship him 'in spirit and in truth.' Without the water of worship to moisten the Word, the seed will not germinate. Fourth, worship intensifies the feeling of God's nearness. The psalmist said, 'O magnify the LORD with me.' To magnify means to make larger. When one hundred people are worshiping God, the sinner sees God one hundred times greater.

"And last," Tommy continued, "true worship creates freedom in the service. 'Where the Spirit of the Lord is, there is liberty.' Our hand clapping, hallelujahs, and shouts of praise bring an atmosphere of deliverance and make it easier for the seeker to go to the altar. Our worship is contagious. This is why, Steve, in our church, worship is not an option. I insist upon it. My people know I'm not going to let them coast through a service as if it were unimportant. The presence of Jesus is too precious for that.

"I also require them to back up the preaching. This is also a type of worship. You see, Steve, the Word is a two-edged sword. It cuts deep into the heart of a sinner. Paul said, 'The letter killeth, but the spirit giveth life.' Our worship can't stop once the preaching starts. It's Spirit-filled worship that helps the Word remove the cancer of sin without killing the sinner. It also brings a unity of minds and hearts into the Word. All of this creates a revival atmosphere in which God can move."

Steve interrupted. "What do you mean by 'insisting' on their worship?"

"I mean that I refuse to let the church have just an 'ordinary' service. If my people are not getting their minds on God, shutting out everything else and lifting Jesus up, then we'll stop the service until they do. If I have to shut the whole service down and send them back to the prayer room, I will. I've done it before, and I'll do it again. I don't have to worry about God doing His part if only we will do our part. That's why I preach, 'If it is to be, it is up to me.' Worship is the key, friend, that will transform an ordinary service into an extraordinary service."

Leaning back, Steve took a deep breath and let it out slowly. "I have much to learn, Pastor. But I think I've learned something tonight that will benefit me and my church for a long, long time. Many men have told me *who* to have for revival. You are the first to explain *how* to have revival. I heard a proverb once that went something like this: If you give a man a fish, you feed him for a day; but if you teach him how to fish, you feed him for a lifetime. Thank you, you've blessed my soul tonight."

As Steve stepped into his car following his visit, he paused and looked up into the clear, cloudless night. A wash of stars glittered behind a full moon. "Lord," he whispered, "forgive me. Forgive me for ever doubting You. And thank You for giving me a second chance."

With that prayer, he started the car, pulled onto the country road, and headed back to Elder Keller's house.

Chapter Nine

The Church Growth Spiral

Steve awoke early the next morning with the sound of rain thundering steadily upon the roof. Off in the distance the muffled echoes of thunder rumbled like remote cannons upon a battlefield. Through the window, fingers of lightning sparked erratically against the low, somber sky. Tiny branches scratched the shingles overhead as the wind pulled the old tree first one way then another.

Steve lay listening to the wintery sounds and enjoying the thick, musty smell of dampness that old houses have during a storm. He had just snuggled deeper beneath the warm, layered quilts when the thought struck him: he had left the windows down in his car.

Leaping out of bed, he grabbed his robe, wrapping it awkwardly around him as he dashed out the bedroom door, and ran down the stairs two at a time. He was halfway outside before Elder Keller called him up short.

"Hold up, son! I already got them."

"Got what, the windows?" Steve asked incredulously, holding onto the door with one hand and his robe with the other, still ready to dash into the drenching downpour.

"That's right," Brother Keller replied. "I woke up when it first started around five this morning. I noticed you left the windows down when you drove in last night."

"You were awake?" asked Steve.

"Off and on. I don't sleep too soundly anymore. Now close the door. Can't afford to heat the whole neighborhood."

The old pastor was standing in the darkened living room before a crackling fire. Lazarus lay by his feet. The old dog hadn't opened an eye in spite of the commotion.

Steve shut the door with a sheepish grin. "Well, thanks. I forgot to roll them up. The sky was so clear last night."

It was then that he noticed with surprise that the elderly pastor leaned heavily on a cane. "Are you hurt, sir?"

Elder Keller shrugged. "Not really. It's my knee. Arthritis acts up in wet weather. I'll be fine by tomorrow. Hurry and get your shower. I need to be at the church by 8:30, and I want you to go with me."

"Why so early?"

"I'm speaking to the kids in chapel this morning at the Christian school. Afterwards I want to discuss some more material. We have some sizable territory yet to cover." Steve was halfway up the stairs when Brother Keller called after him. "And don't forget your notebook. You'll be doing some more writing today."

Our Goals Are Souls

Steve thoroughly enjoyed the morning chapel and especially Elder Keller's message. That the students loved the old man of God was obvious. They sat like watchful little soldiers in rapt attention from the moment he took the floor.

The old pastor's title and text, A Time to Laugh and a Time to Cry, set the stage from the beginning for twenty minutes of funny stories about pioneer Pentecostals. However, the final story was a touching account of the old pastor's crippled brother, whom the Lord had miraculously healed. When Brother Keller concluded, not a dry eye remained, Pastor Martin's included. Chapel went overtime that day.

When the two men finally left it was late morning. The rain had slackened some, but still fell in a steady drizzle, the wind whipping swirling gusts through the open door. They walked back across the brick courtyard, umbrellas in hand, and entered the side door into the quiet sanctuary.

As the older man held the door for the younger, a shaft of light gleamed through the door and fell upon the back wall of the dark auditorium, bringing to Steve's attention the large display case mounted there. He had noticed it the night before as he sat on the platform. The slogan "OUR GOALS ARE SOULS" stood out in bold, red letters across the top. Now he walked over to examine it more closely.

"What's this, Elder?" he asked as Brother Keller came to stand beside him.

Centered with the glass-fronted case was a four-sided chart of some sort. Lines, numbers, and boxes were neatly arranged in a curious, symmetrical balance. Below the red slogan, the title "Church Growth Spiral" had been carefully painted on a poster-board placard. Many of the tiny, two-inch squares, sixteen on each side, had plastic numbers carefully arranged within. At the bottom of the chart, four thermometer-style bar graphs hung, partially filled in with red ribbon. It looked as if a great deal of effort and time had gone into the chart's construction, yet for the life of him, Steve couldn't figure out what it meant. (See figure 12.)

Figure 12

"Our Goals Are Souls"

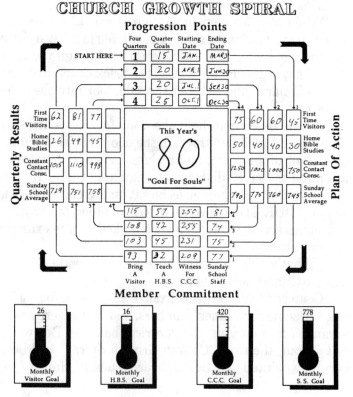

"That's our Church Growth Spiral board," the old pastor replied in a matter-of-fact tone.

Steve grinned. "Oh, sure. I should have known. Now, uh . . . what is it?"

"It's the way we set our evangelism goals and help motivate our people to reach them. Come on, I'll tell you about it later after we discuss some other things first."

The young pastor stood unmoving, staring at the Church Growth Spiral with both hands on hips. "But how does it work?" he pressed. "Just explain it quickly. You've sparked my curiosity. I've never seen anything like it."

Elder Keller started to argue, then shrugged his shoulders in resignation. "All right, but quickly—we're short of time. You remember your first day here we talked about setting five-year number goals?"

Steve nodded. "Sure. You had me so charged up I couldn't sleep."

"Well, the growth spiral is a tool to help you reach your five-year goals. We are on year three of our five-year growth plan to reach one thousand. Our Sunday school goal this year is 790. Our adult goal is to add forty new, solid members. To do this (figuring a fifty-percent retention factor) we need at least eighty adults to receive the Holy Ghost by year's end. It's this number we put in the center box of the spiral, the one labeled 'This Year's Goal for Souls.'"

This Year's

80

"Goal For Souls"

"We then take that goal of eighty and divide it into the four quarters of the year. However, instead of four equal parts, we make each quarter a little larger than the previous one. Can you remember why?"

"Sure," Steve replied, raising one finger in the air and turning his eyes upward in mocking quote: "To give it a slight progressive progression, because you'll be larger the last quarter of the year than you will the first and therefore able to do more. New converts produce more new converts." He looked back at Elder Keller, grinning. "Right?"

"Wise guy, huh?" the old pastor replied dryly. "Didn't anyone ever tell you it's not polite to quote someone without permission? Anyway, that gave us our goal for each quarter. The four quarters add up to our annual goal of eighty."

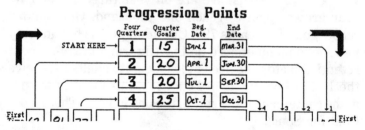

CHURCH GROWTH SPIRAL
Progression Points

	Four Quarters	Quarter Goals	Beg. Date	End Date
START HERE →	1	15	Jan 1	Mar.31
	2	20	Apr. 1	Jun.30
	3	20	Jul. 1	Sep.30
	4	25	Oct.1	Dec.31

"Then," he continued, "we put the beginning and ending dates for each quarter. Now, Mr. Einstein, you remember why it's important to set dates for your goals?"

"Yes, sir. May I quote you again? You said, 'A goal is not a goal until a date is put upon it. A goal without a date is only a dream.' "

"Now you've got it. So this entire top section, which you see is labeled 'Progression Points,' covers the first two steps of proper goal setting: first set your goal, then break that goal into progression points. Understand?"

"Sure," said Steve. "Keep going."

He could see that Brother Keller, in spite of his feigned irritation, was enjoying himself. Steve leaned back against a pew as the older pastor began to warm to his subject.

"All right, you see that the spiral travels in a clockwise direction. It starts with the outer-edge squares and spirals in toward your center goal. Following the arrows takes us to the second section, the Plan Of Action. Here you see listed the four primary outreach methods used at Apostolic Tabernacle: bringing visitors, teaching home Bible studies, personal witnessing (we use a little program called Constant Contact Consciousness to encourage this), and finally, Sunday school. These four methods are the key to the spiral's effectiveness."

"Why those four?"

"Let me explain it like this. Remember the large oak tree in the courtyard? The one where the picnic table was sitting?"

"Yes, sir."

"Here." The elderly pastor reached inside his pocket and withdrew a slender, pearl-handled penknife. "Take my pocketknife and go cut that old tree down. When you get it cut down, come back and tell me."

Steve laughed, "No way. It would take forever."

"It would, wouldn't it?" The old pastor's face was serious.

"I . . . I guess so, but if I'm to cut down a tree, sir, I'll use a chain saw."

"My point exactly. If you're going to do a job, son, you should use the most effective tools possible. Unfortunately, when it comes to outreach programs, Pentecost has seen its share of pocketknives. However, we also have some chain saws. You know what I mean?"

Steve paused to consider before answering. "I think so. You're saying that some evangelistic methods win more souls than do others."

The old man nodded. "Several years ago I took a long, hard look at our outreach program. We had all kinds of people involved in all kinds of ministries: door knocking, street services, Bible studies, bus ministry, rest homes, tract passing, and so on. Yet, for the hours spent, we saw meager results. After a while, that becomes discouraging.

"So," he continued, "I resolved to do some research on my own. I wanted to find what methods were bringing in the most souls. We decided to ask all new converts several questions: who won them to God, how had they been contacted, what led them to see their need, and so on. I typed up six questions. I conducted this survey for one year, and I asked several pastor friends to do the same. When our figures were tallied, four methods stood out overwhelmingly over all others. I don't think it was a coincidence that they all had strong biblical support, either.

Key Concept Ten

**Thou shalt inspire thy people to sow
My Word continually according to the pattern
I have given thee within the Book.**

"The most productive method of evangelism was attracting first-time visitors to church services. You see, son, your church services are your most effective tool of evangelism. Paul said, 'How shall they hear without a preacher?' and 'It pleased God by the foolishness of preaching to save them that believe.' There is tremendous power in anointed preaching. It will convict a sinner's heart faster than anything else. The public service is also the most prevalent tool of evangelism in the New Testament. Why is it so effective? Because a person will feel more of God in an apostolic service than anywhere else. The key is getting them there.

"Now, I've been criticized by some because I have so many special services: revivals, singspirations, guest speakers, missionaries, dramas, training seminars, and so on. But I've found that the more opportunities we provide people to invite folks, the more visitors we have. And the more visitors we have, the more conversions we see. So we plan various special services throughout the year and strongly encourage our members to invite friends and relatives. It takes considerable work and planning, but it pays off."

Steve sat quietly nodding his head and taking this all in. Now he scowled. "Wait a minute, Elder. That's fine for you. You have a large church. But we can barely pay our bills. We can't afford what you're doing."

"Steve," Brother Keller replied, "don't misunderstand me. I'm not saying you should continually schedule special services—and please don't think we do either. Oh, I guess we have more than average, yet the number's small when compared to our regular services. What I am saying is this: since visitors are your best outreach, it stands to reason that you should offer something when they come. That's why it's vital to have a move of God in every service, not just during special services. *Every* service should be special."

"Oh," Steve responded, "I see what you're saying. Tommy talked about the same thing last night: the importance of having a revival atmosphere every time we have church."

"Right," Elder Keller said, his eyes sparkling, for this was his favorite subject. "But when you do have a special service, promote it *big*. Push for all the visitors you can get. It's your key outreach. Print up fliers, post posters, advertise in the newspaper, get commitments from your people to bring friends, and most importantly, fast and pray. Don't just have a two-week meeting, have a Holy Ghost Crusade, a Miracle Meeting, an Endtime Explosion. Appoint a revival committee to help develop new ideas. Take Solomon's advice: 'Whatsoever thy hand findeth to do, do it with thy might.' Your church should be the most exciting place in town."

"Okay," Steve replied, "so first-time visitors are definitely a chain saw. Any others?"

Brother Keller pointed at the board. "The second most effective method we found was home Bible study. This method is also strongly supported by the New Testament. The early Christians taught 'daily in the temple, and in every house.' Paul said to the Ephesian elders, 'I . . . have taught you publickly, and from house to house.' If people will not come to *us* to hear the gospel, we must take it to *them*. What home Bible study does is increase the number of visitors you will have who are hungry for salvation. Your altars will never be empty if your people will teach Bible studies. It is the most effective tool or program we have outside of church services. Having an active, effective Bible study ministry in your church should be one of your highest priorities."

Steve nodded for Elder Keller to continue.

"The third most effective method was personal witnessing. If you can get your people to give their personal testimony—to tell how the Lord saved them—you will have more Bible studies and visitors both. And I don't mean getting into a scriptural debate or argument, either. Too many times folks beat someone over the head with the Bible and walk away thinking, I sure told them, when all they did was tell them off.

"The Apostle Paul attended some of the finest schools of his day. He was no dummy. Yet we find him giving the account of his conversion more often than any other message. I have discovered that people can argue with my theology, but they can't argue with my testimony. They can't argue that I spoke in tongues, that I was healed, that I was delivered from liquor, that I have joy and peace. Our personal testimony is the most powerful tool we have. If you can get your people to share it, your results will be dramatic."

"But," Steve interrupted, "how do you get people to witness more?"

"Well, it's not as hard as you might think. First, you need to teach your members how to witness properly and share the truth. The 'Fisherman's Workshop' is an excellent training course for this purpose.[2] Then, encourage them to develop a lifestyle of personal witnessing. Witnessing must become a good habit just as daily prayer must become a good habit. To do this we use a little ministry called Constant Contact Consciousness.[3] It helps people become constantly conscious of the need to contact people for the Lord."

Steve shook his head dolefully. "You know, Elder, the sad fact is, many people will go for weeks without witnessing to anyone."

"Exactly," Brother Keller replied. "And they never think about it until you preach a message on soul winning. Then they'll repent and do fine for a few days but soon fall back into the same rut. Constant Contact Consciousness is a weekly reminder of their witnessing efforts. Most people tell me they need that reminder. It's not that people don't want to witness, it's that they forget. We try to get almost all the church participating. What it's done is develop a soul-consciousness in our people wherever they go."

"Sounds great," Steve responded. "I want to get some more details on it before I leave. But tell me about your last method, Elder. It surprises me. I've never thought of Sunday school as an outreach. As I said, in our church it's mainly an educational program for the kids."

"I know, son, and you need to change that. The largest denominations in America will tell you that Sunday school is the greatest arm of evangelism they have. It's a proven fact that at least fifty percent of your Sunday school enrollment will attend regularly. If you'll increase your enrollment, you'll increase your attendance."

"But," Steve inquired, "how can I increase my Sunday school enrollment apart from conversions?"

"Through an enrollment campaign.[4] You see, Steve, Americans, because of their Puritan heritage, feel a deep need to belong to some religious faith. They will enroll in a Sunday school even though they only attend occasionally. However, let them experience a traumatic crisis in their life—death, divorce, jail, illness, so on—and they'll come running to God for help. If they are enrolled in Sunday school, it will be to your altars they run. And when they receive the Holy Ghost, they make first-class saints.

"Of course," the old pastor continued, "we also use the revised method of bus ministry Tommy told you about yeterday. Once we have the children in Sunday school, we have a good chance of getting a Bible study in the home. We also use the monthly Holy Ghost Sunday to increase conversions in our classes. That, along with our Kamp Kid Krusade, results in a large percentage of children being saved."

"Kamp Kid Krusade?" Steve said with a smile. "What's that?"

"That's our promotion to inspire church members to sponsor bus children for youth camp. Most of the children come back from camp with the Holy Ghost. And when a child receives the Holy Ghost, we almost always get a Bible study in the parent's home."

Steve leaned his head back and began to laugh softly. "You guys don't miss a lick, do you?" he said, still grinning.

"Young man, the Lord's coming. We can't afford to. Jesus commanded us to go into the highways and byways and compel them. I feel that Sunday school is a direct fulfillment of that commission."

The young man glanced at Brother Keller. He was leaning heavily upon his cane, his arthritic knee carefully bent so as to carry no weight. Steve reached over, picked up an usher's chair, and set it down in the aisle before the spiral board. With a gleam in his eye, he pointed to it and said, "Sit down, Elder. The more I hear about this growth spiral, the more interested I get. I'm not leaving until you explain how these four methods work along with this spiral thing of yours."

The Church Growth Spiral

Sighing softly, the old man eased into the seat. "Son, I hadn't planned to get into this today."

"I know, sir," Steve said, grinning, "but this is so fascinating I couldn't concentrate on anything else anyway. If you didn't want questions you shouldn't have hung it on the wall."

The older man smiled too. "You do have a point."

He continued. "The growth spiral, Steve, encourages these four methods by showing you roughly what needs to be done within each to see a given result—in this case, your quarterly new convert goals. It's not enough to say 'Church, our goal is to bring a bunch of visitors, teach a heap of Bible studies, and witness to oodles of people.'' Heaps and oodles are not goals. To be a goal, it must be specific, measurable, and tangible. However, the sixty-four dollar question is this: how many visitors must be brought, how many Bible studies must be taught, and how many contacts must be made to obtain the new convert goals? The way to answer the question is by a simple equation based upon statistical averages. For visitors it is three times the quarterly goal. What was our first quarter's goal son?"

"Fifteen."

"And what's three times fifteen?"

"Forty-five."

"So, how many first-time visitors needed to walk through our doors between January 1 and March 31?"

"Forty-five!" Steve exclaimed excitedly.

"Sure. So that was our goal. We had to reach at least that many. And we had no problem doing it because that's less than four visitors each week. With a church our size, that was easy. Now the second quarter's goal went up to sixty (three times twenty). The third quarter's goal was sixty also, and the last quarter's goal is seventy-five (three times twenty-five), which is still only six visitors per week."

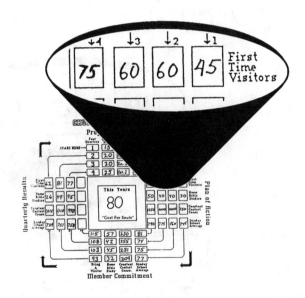

"I see!" Steve injected. "So you get your people to commit to that goal and then you push and promote it all quarter."

"You're catching on. Now with home Bible studies, the equation is two times the quarterly goal. So how many Bible studies needed to be taught the first quarter?"

"Thirty, because two times fifteen is thirty."

"Right," Elder Keller nodded, "and with almost three hundred adults in our church, we were more than capable of doing that. Fact is, we got that many from our visitor follow-up ministry. Now, the second quarter's goal for Bible studies was forty (two times twenty). The same for the third quarter, and the last quarter's goal is fifty (two times twenty-five)."

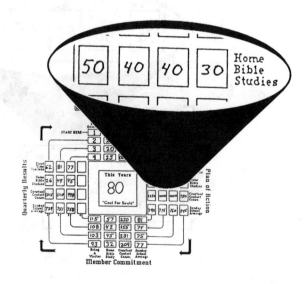

   "Now Constant Contact Consciousness is the number of personal testimonies given by our members. Those involved in this ministry turn in a simple report slip of their contacts so that we can track our progress. The equation here is fifty times the quarterly goal. Fifty times fifteen is 750, which was the total contacts we needed to have that first quarter. That was only around sixty contacts per week. We socked that number out of the ball park. The goal for the second and third quarters was 1,000, and the last quarter's goal is 1,250."

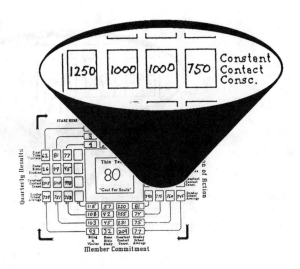

"With Sunday school," he continued, "we don't need an equation, because our five-year plan has already set our attendance goal for this year. We need an average of 790 in Sunday school by the end of December (a goal of 60 over our last year's average, which was 730). So when we divided the 60 into the four quarters, we saw that we needed to increase our attendance by 15 people each quarter. So our goal for the first quarter was 745 (730 + 15). The second was 760, the third was 775, and our final quarterly goal for Sunday school is 790. Follow me?"

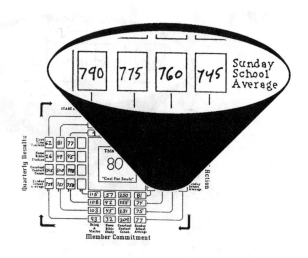

"I think so," Steve said slowly, staring at the chart before him. "Does that Sunday school goal represent an average for the entire quarter?"

"No. We try to average those numbers during the final month of each quarter. The last four or five Sundays should average close to our quarterly goal."

Steve nodded. As long as he watched the chart, it all made sense. "So your outreach goals for the first quarter were forty-five first-time visitors, thirty home Bible studies, 750 contacts, and a 745 average in Sunday school."

"Right. You see, son," the older man explained, making a broad sweep with his hand toward the bulletin board, "the power of the spiral lies in getting your people to focus upon what is *their* responsibility instead of *God's* responsibility. You see this year's goal of eighty to get the Holy Ghost? We can't do that."

"What?" Steve said with surprise, "What do you mean you can't do it? I thought that was your goal!"

"No, sir. Can *you* give anyone the Holy Ghost?"

"Well . . . no."

"Therefore, it can't be your goal. What good is a goal that you have no control over? That's God's goal. He's the only one who can give the Holy Ghost. I can get excited about it, but that number is completely out of my hands. He didn't tell us to give folks the Holy Ghost, He told us to sow seed. The very essence of the verse 'He that goeth forth, and weepeth, bearing precious seed, shall doubtless come again with rejoicing, bringing his sheaves with him' is this: if we will do *our* job, God will do *His* job. So I just laid it on the line. I said, 'Church, are you willing to do your part? It's the law of the harvest: we

219

will only reap what we have sown. If we sow sparingly, we will reap sparingly. But if we sow abundantly, we will reap abundantly. So church, will you commit with me to reach these goals?' And they did. Thus far, we're doing great."

"But," Steve responded, "what if you reach all your outreach goals the first quarter, and you only have, let's say, eight receive the Holy Ghost. Your goal was fifteen. What then?"

"That's fine, because how many get the Holy Ghost is up to God. We might do everything the second quarter also and only see ten adults saved. We might do everything the third quarter and see a *hundred* and ten saved! Son, when it's harvest time, it's harvest time!"

Elder Keller struggled to his feet, one bony finger pointing upward, his eyes flashing with inner zeal. "You can't make God a computer, young man, plugging numbers in here and seeing results come out there. You can only do your best and trust Him for the rest."

The old pastor jabbed his finger in Steve's direction. "The problem is, most pastors frustrate their people by setting goals over which they have no control. They set a goal for a certain number to be saved, and when their people don't see results, they become discouraged. Not this preacher! Paul said, 'Let us not be weary in well doing: for in due season we shall reap, if we faint not.' So when the end of the quarter comes and we see we've reached our outreach goals, we shout the walls down! We have a spirit of victory and the joy of success. Don't worry about God. He'll do his part; just give Him time!" And with that, he collapsed—that's the only word for it—back down into his seat.

Steve stared at the spiral chart in front of him. His face was a curious mixture of excitement and surprise. After a moment, he said one word: "Wow."

Then he said it again as the full power of the spiral began to sink in slowly. Finally he turned around to face Brother Keller, his face glowing like a boy with a new puppy, one fist beating the air over his head. "It'll work! I know it'll work! Brother Keller, this is what I've been needing! Man, oh, man! Where have you been all my life?" Steve began to pace back and forth, his face painted with a faraway look. "I can do it, Elder. In five years, I can be running three hundred. No, make that four hundred! There's no doubt in my mind. If I can just get my people committed to doing their part." The young pastor paused and stopped short. "That's the key, isn't it? Getting everybody committed?"

"Yes, my young friend," Elder Keller said, a grin stretching from ear to ear, "that is the key. Two or three people can't do it all. It will require a total effort. And that brings us to the third part of the spiral, the part labeled 'member commitment.'

"The spiral," he explained, "requires a commitment service to be held each year. I always held ours during watch-night service. I explained our five-year goals for Sunday school, members, and new converts. Then I plugged that year's number into the spiral and showed them what needed to be done on our part if we expected God to do his. I usually preached hard on the need to win the lost and our own personal responsibility for involvement. Then I handed out a commitment card and had everyone check off where they were willing to be involved that first quarter. Some checked only one ministry; others checked all four. I encouraged them to do as much as they could. They then signed the card and handed it back. The totals were posted on this spiral bulletin board. You can see on the board that this year we had 93 promise to bring a visitor that first quarter, 32 to teach a Bible study, 209 to be involved in C.C.C. and 77 to work in the Sunday school and bus ministry.''

Member Commitment

"So," Steve questioned, "each quarter they will recommit to their involvement?''

"Exactly. Then at the end of each quarter, we will post what we have *actually* done. These results are placed in the last section of the spiral, which is labeled 'Quarterly Results.' You can see that our results were 62 first-time visitors, 26 Bible studies taught, 1,015 contacts made and a Sunday school average for March of 744.''

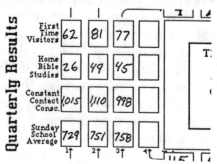

"But," Steve said, pointing to the results area, "you missed your goal in Bible studies and Sunday school."

"Well, Sunday school was close enough that we let it pass. However, home Bible study was another thing. We missed our goal of thirty studies by four. An excellent benefit of the growth spiral is evaluation. Each quarter you see where your weaknesses are so that you can work on them. Son, you and I both know that whatever the pastor pushes works better."

The young man nodded.

"Well, that following quarter, Tommy strongly pushed Bible studies. He urged more involvement and asked for more studies to be taught. We got both. Yet, come the third quarter, our Sunday school growth was down, so we had to work on that. Whatever is weak, that's what you focus upon. This helps your outreach program to stay in balance. In the world they call it a good marketing mix.

"Then, at the start of each quarter, on a Bible study night, we hold a special spiral promotion service. Here we review our results, have testimonies about our success, preach on soul winning, and ask people to stand and recommit in each area. We always try to get more people involved in the four key ministries. It's an exciting service, because people can visually *see* the fruit of their labors. Do you follow what I'm saying?"

The young man was nodding his head. "I sure do, sir, and I can see why the spiral is such a powerful motivational tool."

"Yes, it is. It involves every step of effective goal setting: set your goal, break it into progression points, work out your plan of action, develop your resources, and evaluate your results. It's all there. But don't forget that's all it is—a goal-setting tool—not a magic formula for instant success. The law of the harvest requires more than just going forth and bearing precious seed. It also requires weeping. If you allow this plan to become only numbers, it will fail. It must be accompanied by prayer, fasting, burdens, and tears."

The young man nodded his head solemnly. "Elder, I must show this to my church. Do you have this on paper? Something that I can take with me?"

"Yes, son, I have one I'll give you. But why don't we pray for a while first? For some reason, I feel the Lord very close right now."

The young man stood and followed the old pastor down the center aisle to the front of the church. There, for the next hour, they knelt together and talked to God.

Chapter Ten

Constant Contact Consciousness

After prayer, Brother Keller ushered Steve into Tommy's office. Motioning for the young man to sit on the sofa, the old man eased himself carefully down into the soft desk chair. Tenderly he stretched out his stiff leg beside the desk to rest on a low footstool. He was smiling weakly, but Steve could see the pain written upon his face.

Frowning with concern he asked, "Is there something I can get you, sir? Would you rather go home and rest? Look, don't worry about me. We can get together another time."

"No, Steve," Brother Keller replied in a steady, quiet tone, "I can't let a thing like this stop me. I may be old, but I'm not foolish. If I were looking for an excuse to slow down or quit, the devil could give me plenty. Life is full of difficulties and obstacles. A person who is going to work for God must learn to ignore the problems and press on anyway. Somewhere the Bible says, 'He that observeth the wind shall not sow; and he that regardeth the clouds shall not reap.' In other words, if you wait for conditions to be perfect, you will get nothing done."

"I understand, sir, but I hate to see you suffering so."

"Ah!" the old pastor growled, waving his hand in mock disgust. "Don't worry about me. I'll be all right." He adjusted himself a bit more comfortably. "Now," he continued, "you wanted to work out a growth spiral. Let me see what I can find."

The old pastor pulled out the desk file drawer and began to flip through it. "I don't see anything here. Let me call Jo Ann. She should have one filed somewhere in the front office." A few minutes later Jo Ann gave them a copy.[1]

"Now," the old pastor continued, "do you remember how many need to receive the Holy Ghost this next year from your five-year plan?"

"Yes, sir. I want twelve new adult members. Figuring a fifty-percent retention average, I'll need at least twenty-four to receive the Holy Ghost this next year."

"Fine. Write that number in the center box. Now, divide that number into four quarterly goals, giving them a slight progressive progression."

Steve started to write, then paused. "Isn't there an easier way to figure that progressive progression than just to guess at it?"

"Sure, you have a pocket calculator?"

"Uh . . . there's one on the desk, sir."

"Oh . . . right. Well, multiply your center goal by twenty-two percent for the first quarter, twenty-four percent for the second quarter, twenty-six percent for the third and twenty-eight percent for the last quarter. These add up to one hundred percent, or your total goal."

Steve quickly punched the numbers in. "Okay, I have

it. The first quarter is five, the second is six, the third is six also, and the last quarter's seven. I rounded the numbers up or down so they would equal twenty-four."

"Fine," he said. "Now write in each quarter's date—got it? All right, now use your four equations to come up with each quarter's outreach goals."

"Wait a minute, sir," Steve interrupted, holding up his hand. "I have a question. I know you said these four methods have proven to be the most productive, but what about my other ministries? Do I drop them for these alone? Is there a way to add them to the spiral?"

"Depends," the elder replied. "Are your other outreaches bringing results? I know that sounds harsh; however, you only have so many people. If they are tied to an outreach that never produces, or produces little for the time involved, then I'd let it go. Your methods must be continually evaluated to see if they help you reach your goals. Many fall into the trap of confusing activity with accomplishment. Never simply ask, Am I doing something? Rather ask, What am I doing? and Is it producing results? Marry the message, my friend, but never go steady with a method."

"But what if it *is* producing? Can I add it to the spiral?"

"Steve, the spiral is simply a tool. It can be altered to fit any situation. Some churches don't have a Sunday school, so they substituted another ministry in its place. Others find the equations lie far below what they're currently doing—they might have more visitors than three times the quarterly goal, so they raise it to four or five times to give their people a worthwhile challenge. As long as the equation is raised instead of lowered, it will not harm your results. The key to the spiral's success is consistency, commitment, and evaluation. If you will work your most productive ministries on a consistent basis, get your people committed to involvement, and evaluate your results regularly, you can't help but see results. However, an erratic, half-hearted effort will rarely bear fruit. So to answer your question: yes, you can add a ministry to the spiral and develop your own equation for its goals. But let me caution you to not make the spiral too complicated. Don't spread the focus too widely or it will lose its punch."

Steve nodded. "I see your point, sir. I think I'll leave it as it is for now. That way I'll know better how it works."

"I think that's wise," Brother Keller agreed. "Now let's set your outreach goals. How many visitors will you need each quarter?"

"Well, at three times the quarterly goal, I'll need fifteen the first quarter, eighteen the second quarter, eighteen the third, and twenty-one the last."

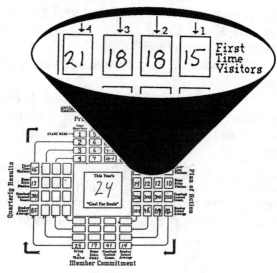

"Is that realistic?" Brother Keller asked. "Can your people bring that many visitors out to church?"

"We should, sir. We have one, maybe two visitors a week now. Although that last quarter will make us stretch, hopefully the excitement will catch on."

"Good. The last several quarters should make you stretch. If you do no more than what you're doing now, what benefit is that? Now, for this to be most effective, you need to have an aggressive visitor follow-up ministry. Do you have one?"

Roll Out the Red Carpet

Steve looked puzzled. "I'm not sure what you mean. I try to send each visitor a card or something when they sign the guest book, or perhaps I should say *if* they sign the guest book. I haven't had much luck in that area."

Brother Keller dropped one bushy eyebrow in disapproval. "Son, you need to realize that your best prospects are those who walk through the church doors. Too often we keep reaching for more and practically ignore the ones we get. That's like getting a fish on one line, then ignoring it to cast for another. Research has proven that those who receive the Holy Ghost usually come between three and five times before they finally go to the altar. What that means is this: if you're going to have many new converts, you have to get that visitor back a second and third time. A good visitor follow-up ministry will go far in helping them return."

"But," Steve argued, "I've had some get the Holy Ghost the first time they came!"

"And how long did they stay?"

"Oh . . . now that you mention it, not too long."

229

"My point exactly. Many who receive the Holy Ghost or are baptized their first time in a Pentecostal service go out as easily as they came in. I would rather that people came back several times and truly make up their mind to live for God. That kind will stick. But, remember, even if they don't go to the altar, they feel the touch of the Spirit. Also, most have an interest in God, or they wouldn't have come. You need to roll out the red carpet to make visitors feel that this is the finest church in town."

"How do you suggest?"

"Many ways. Let me give you an example. Several years ago my wife and I were on vacation in another state. It was a church night, so we decided to visit a neighboring church totally unannounced. On the way there, we stopped to eat at a local restaurant. As we pulled into the parking lot, an attendant showed us a convenient space and graciously assisted us out of the car and up to the entrance. A doorkeeper met us, shook our hand, and opened the door. We were then welcomed by a charming hostess, who showed us to a table. Soon, a friendly waitress greeted us and took our order. The meal was excellent. As we left, the maitre d' smiled warmly, asked if all was well, and wished us a pleasant evening.

"We then traveled a short distance to the church. No one met us in the parking lot or even greeted us at the door. We found our own seat and suffered through a dead, dry service (yes, it was Pentecostal). At the conclusion, no one greeted us or wished us well, except for the pastor, and even he was lukewarm." The old man of God paused and shook his head sadly. "Had they both offered an invitation, I would have joined the restaurant."[2]

The young man sat chuckling as the old man went

on. "It is a sad reproach when the church of the living God is any less appealing or friendly than a place of business. When visitors come to our church, they are met by a parking-lot attendant who directs them to a special section reserved for visitors. They are then met at the door by a doorkeeper who shakes their hand and asks them if they have filled out a guest card. If not, he will introduce them to one of our hostesses. She will help them fill out the card and give them our visitor's packet. She in turn introduces them to one of our ushers. The usher will help them find a seat on the main aisle about halfway down. Our members have been well instructed to move to the center if an aisle seat is needed for a visitor. As the usher seats them, he will introduce several families sitting nearby. The names and locations of all visitors are taken to the pastor once service begins. He will personally greet them from the pulpit."

"My!" Steve said, his voice full of admiration. "Now that's what I call being made welcome. But doesn't that require a lot of people?"

"What I just described involves four people: lot attendant, doorkeeper, hostess, and usher. Of course, in a church our size they work in pairs. But in a smaller church, that wouldn't be necessary. A key reason behind the entire process is to ensure that we get a guest card. Once we have a guest card, we can then plug them into the four steps of our visitor follow-up program."

"Which are?" asked Steve.

"First, all guest cards are photocopied four times. One copy goes to Sister Boothe who calls them the next day. She says something like, 'Hi, this is Sister Boothe from Apostolic Tabernacle. Pastor Keller asked me to call and let you know how much we appreciated your visiting with us this last Sunday. If there is anything else we can do for you, please let us know.' It's simple and short but carries a powerful message of love and concern.

"The second copy goes to Brother Barentine, our visitor follow-up coordinator. He will assign someone to drop by that week. The main purpose of the visit is to tell them about our home Bible study program. If we can get them in a Bible study, we'll normally get them in our altars. The third copy goes to Jo Ann, our church secretary. She will send them a personal letter from the pastor inviting them back. Then the last copy will go to Sister Moore, our public relations director. She will add their names to the church mailing list. All our visitors receive our monthly news bulletin for one year. Using bulk mailing, the cost is minimal, yet it promotes upcoming events and reminds them of the wonderful touch they felt when they attended."

"How do you keep everything going, Elder? I tried once to start a follow-up system in my church. But unless I did it, it fell apart."

"Organizing a ministry is only half the job, Steve. Remember, I told you that organization will not work without management. That's why I established a separate department called Visitor Follow-Up. The director goes to the retreat, hands in a one-year plan, and attends the monthly council and weekly tag-in. That's what keeps the ministry going. He also hands in a weekly and monthly status report. So when problems develop, we can fix them before they destroy the whole system."

Steve sighed deeply. "You're right, Elder. That's been my problem. Not only with follow-up, but with a lot of other things that have fizzled."

Out of Sight, Out of Mind

"We live and learn, my friend. Now, let's see your goals for home Bible study. How many studies will you need to reach your quarterly goals?"

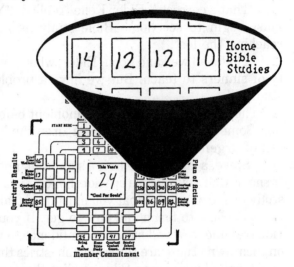

"Uh. . . ," Steve scratched his head. "The equation is two times the quarterly goal, isn't it? So I'll need ten the first quarter, twelve the second, twelve the third, and fourteen the fourth. Now another question: do these Bible studies have to be completed to be counted?"

"Well, we both know that not everyone who starts a Bible study completes it, although I think at least two or three lessons should be taught to even say you gave a good try. Now, remember, these are Bible studies to sinners, not saints. All new converts need a Bible study,

233

but we're focusing upon evangelism here, not discipleship."

"So, you're saying that if someone is saved through a revival or personal witnessing, and they have never had a Bible study, the study taught them for discipleship purposes would not be included in your spiral results?"

"That's correct," Elder Keller replied. "Your people must begin to see home Bible study as a method of reaching the lost."

"That's all well and good, Elder, when you have plenty of sinners to teach. But we have a problem getting studies."

The old pastor paused for a moment before answering. Somewhere in the distance a siren thinly wailed its call of urgency and concern.

"Steve, a lack of studies is a symptom, not a problem. It shows that your people are not thinking in a home Bible study frame of mind. What you must do is train your people, both how to teach and how to get. If you don't provide training, few will have the confidence to venture out on their own. There are three key ministries that will keep you supplied with more Bible studies than you can ever teach: visitor follow-up, bus ministry, and Saturday door knocking. But if after you have the studies you have no instructors, then your efforts are in vain."

"How do I train them?" Steve queried.

"I suggest two ways. First, plan to have a home Bible study training seminar each year with an outside speaker. This should be taught by someone who has been successful at it himself, for nothing inspires success like success. After the speaker gets your people excited, several nights should be devoted to teaching them how to teach a study and how to get a study. Having a three-night seminar like this every year provides the needed boost to keep the ministry rolling, and it gets your new converts involved. Then you as pastor should teach at least three more training seminars during the remaining twelve months. Space the seminars about four months apart and take two or three evenings to instruct. Encourage everyone who's not teaching a Bible study to attend, especially your new converts. Let your Bible study director help you. And don't make the mistake of just teaching the study to them. Instead, teach them *how* to teach. Keep it moving. The longer you stretch the training out, the fewer people will complete it. If a prospective teacher feels he needs to go through a study, let him assist in one already going. Or have people teach one another, trading every other lesson."

The young pastor bobbed his head in agreement. "Makes sense. Is there anything more I can do?"

"Yes, you also need to promote Bible study regularly. Talk it up. Have your teachers and those they've won testify. Keep the ministry visible. Home Bible study is one of those things that's out of sight out of mind. You must help your people develop a home Bible study mind set."

Constant Contact Consciousness

Steve nodded and made a few notes. "Okay, Elder, now about this Cautious Consistent . . . or whatever you call it."

"Constant Contact Consciousness."

"Right. I never can say it, but I love the idea. What is the equation for that?"

"Fifty times your quarterly goal."

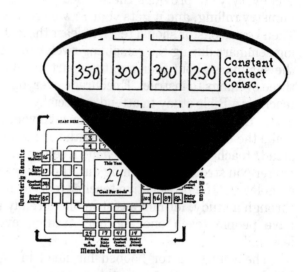

"All right, that would be . . . hmm. . . ," Steve did some quick figuring. "It's 250, for the first quarter, 300 the second quarter, 300 the third and 350 the fourth. Now, how does this tongue twister work? You promised to explain it."

"It's extremely simple. Each Sunday morning my outreach director personally hands to our C.C.C. team (that's what we call those involved—our C.C.C. team) a little slip of paper. On this slip each team member reports his results for the past week. Let me show you one. Tommy should have one around here somewhere." Brother Keller began searching through the desk drawers until he found what he wanted. (See figure 13.)

Figure 13

Constant Contact Consciousness

Name_____Date_____

Number of Contacts This Week_____

"And daily in the temple, and in every
house, they ceased not to TEACH
and PREACH Jesus Christ."

"The team member writes down his name and the number of times he witnessed that week. Now, remember, a contact is more than just inviting someone to church. To be counted, this person must have shared Christ in some meaningful fashion—giving his testimony or explaining salvation. The C.C.C. slip is then dropped in the offering as the plate is passed. My outreach director collects these slips and adds up the contacts. The total is posted each week on the spiral bulletin board."

"I see," Steve responded. "If the person witnessed to a friend or relative he hands in a slip so we can count it toward the spiral goal."

"Yes, but you missed an important point. The C.C.C. team members turn in a slip every week, whether they made any contacts or not. If no contacts, they write down a zero and hand it in."

"Does anyone go and talk to those people? I mean, after all, they didn't keep their commitment to witness each week."

"Never. Because when people commit to C.C.C., they are not committing to witness each week. All they are committing to do is hand in their slip each Sunday, nothing else. Besides, if they haven't given their testimony to anyone, nobody needs to talk to them, the Holy Ghost already has. The Spirit says, 'You mean I gave you seven days, 168 hours, this week, and out of the hundreds of people you met, you couldn't find five minutes to talk to even one person about Me?'"

"Ouch!" Steve said with a wry smile. "That would hurt. Does it seem to work?"

"Friend, it's one of the most effective little ministries we've ever had. It keeps us continually stocked with home Bible studies and visitors. And it's something that everyone, young or old, can be involved in. You see, Steve, only a small percentage of your members will be engaged in Sunday school and bus ministry. Nor is it realistic to think all will teach a Bible study—they just won't. And how many go out to knock on doors? Right now, I would guess that less than ten percent of your church is involved in any kind of organized outreach. What about the other ninety percent? They need some ministry they can be a part of. Constant Contact Consciousness is that type of a ministry.

"I have also found," he continued, "that this ministry is an excellent gauge of the church's spiritual condition. If the totals begin to slip, it's time to preach soul winning again and help the people get a hold of God. When saints are prayed up, they witness. If people will get into the habit of sharing Christ, the Lord will open doors all over."

"Praise God!" Steve exclaimed, smacking his fist into the palm of his hand. "This is exciting! I can't wait to get started, Elder. Why, 750 contacts is nothing. That's only 20 contacts a week. If forty-eight adults can't do that, we all need to pray through."

The old pastor smiled. His student was beginning to catch the vision: growth is not the result of an all-out, back-breaking thrust, but is instead the result of a steady, week-by-week effort, the same way that things grow in the natural world.

"I'm sure," Brother Keller replied, "you can reach them with no trouble. Now let's look at your Sunday school goals. Do you remember how we arrive at them?"

Steve nodded. "My Sunday school goal comes from my five-year plan, right? I take the amount by which I need to grow . . . uh . . . I have it here somewhere." Steve flipped through his notebook quickly. "Here it is. I need to grow by twenty-seven more in average attendance. I then divide that into the four quarters. That would be about seven per quarter. Our average now is seventy-five, so seven plus seventy-five is eighty-two. That," he concluded, looking pleased with himself, "is my first quarter's goal."

"You got it," the old pastor returned, "and the second quarter would be eighty-nine, ninety-six the third, and your last quarter . . . what's your goal for Sunday school next year?"

"One hundred and two, so that would be my last quarter's goal?"

"Right, and the last four Sundays in each quarter,

when averaged together, should reach your quarterly
goal."

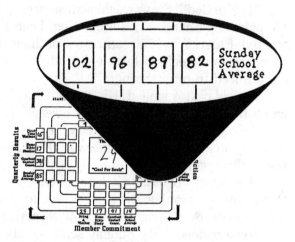

Steve sat back in the chair, the spiral chart grasped
in both hands. "Fifteen visitors, ten home Bible studies,
250 contacts, and eighty-two in Sunday school," he said,
his voice little more than a murmur. He fell quiet for a
moment as he carefully considered each figure. (See figure
14.) Then he continued. "You know, Elder, I'm confident
about reaching every goal here except for home Bible
studies. We only have two, maybe three studies going
now. However, one of those is with a woman who received
the Holy Ghost before she started, so she wouldn't count.
To get ten studies is going to take some doing. I don't
know why, but Bible studies never really caught on in our
church."

Brother Keller didn't reply right away. Instead he
leaned back in his chair, took out his pocketknife, and
began to trim his fingernails. Steve could tell he was reluc-

tant to answer. Finally he came to a decision.

"Steve, let me ask you a straightforward question. In the last five years, how many Bible studies have *you* taught?"

The young man thought for a moment. "Well, you know our church was started with a home Bible study, then the revival I was preaching brought in the rest. I spent the first year or so helping those become established and getting the church going. But in the four years since then, I've probably taught five or six."

"Why so few?"

The young pastor shifted uncomfortably in his seat. It was more an accusation than a question. "Well, I work full time and pastor too. Then a lot of my time is spent preparing to preach, and well, I guess . . ." He trailed off with a downcast look. "I'm . . . I'm sorry, sir. I guess I don't have any real excuse. I always thought that if you could get people to accept truth, come to church, and read their Bibles your church would grow."

"Son, people don't just accept salvation, they must be won. They don't read their Bibles, they must be taught. Nor do they come to church; they must be brought. Jesus didn't tell us to wait for *them* to move, he told *us* to move. You must win them, bring them, teach them. If you don't do it, it won't be done. Your church will see limited growth until you, my friend, are the greatest soul winner there."

Key Concept Eleven

Thou shalt illustrate to thy people the ways of a soul winner, leading them diligently to win the lost.

Steve frowned sullenly. "But I was always told that shepherds don't produce sheep; rather, sheep produce sheep. You know, 'equip the saints' and that sort of thing."

"Young man, never forget that you are first called to be a Christian, secondly a pastor. Your people will not do what you have not been willing to do yourself. No church will rise above the pastor's example. No church will be a soul winning church if the pastor is not a soul winner himself. This is especially true when a church is small or has ceased to grow.

"When I first started pastoring here, I spent many hours each week in personal evangelism. I had to—there was no one else. As the church began to grow, I had to divide my time four ways: as a father and husband, as a breadwinner, as a pastor, and finally, as a soul winner. This last area, son, you must *never* forget, because I found that my being a soul winner was the most powerful people motivator I had. When I would get up to urge my people to win the lost, I could tell them about my Bible study, my door knocking, my visitor follow-up, and those I won to God. It was a rare month when someone didn't pray through as a result of my efforts. The people followed my example. You see, Steve, *if you use the excuse that you're too busy to be a soul winner, then you can expect your people to use the same excuse.*"

Steve stared at the floor for several moments, head bowed, shoulders sagging. The old clock in the corner ticked loudly in the sudden stillness. When he finally looked up, his eyes were glossy.

"You mean, sir, all this time I've been waiting for my people to catch a vision of winning the lost, and the whole time they've been waiting on me to show them how?''

Steve's lip trembled slightly as he shook his head. "O God," he whispered, his voice thick with emotion, "have I ever been a fool! A total complete fool!" He buried his head in his hands.

Slowly the old pastor rose from his chair and hobbled over to the young man, his eyes also spilling over to create shiny streaks upon the wrinkled, aged, skin. Slowly he knelt and wrapped his arm around him, embracing him as one would a young, repentant child. There, in the privacy of Tommy's study, they prayed together for the second time that day.

When Steve arose some time later, something was different inside. He knew with a fixed assurance that his life and his ministry would never be the same.

Figure 14

CHURCH GROWTH SPIRAL

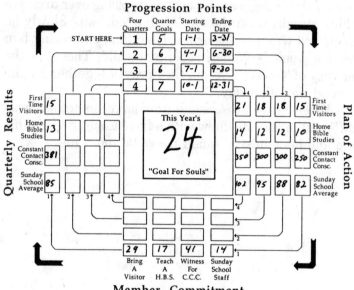

Progression Points

	Four Quarters	Quarter Goals	Starting Date	Ending Date
START HERE →	1	5	1-1	3-31
	2	6	4-1	6-30
	3	6	7-1	9-30
	4	7	10-1	12-31

Quarterly Results

Plan of Action

This Year's **24** "Goal For Souls"

	Quarterly Results					Plan of Action			
First Time Visitors	15					21	18	18	15	First Time Visitors
Home Bible Studies	13					14	12	12	10	Home Bible Studies
Constant Contact Consc.	381					350	300	300	250	Constant Contact Consc.
Sunday School Average	85					102	95	88	82	Sunday School Average

	Bring A Visitor	Teach A H.B.S.	Witness For C.C.C.	Sunday School Staff
	29	17	41	14

Member Commitment

Equations for "Plan of Action" Goals

First Time Visitors . . . . 3 Times the Quarterly Goals
Home Bible Studies . . . . 2 Times the Quarterly Goals
Constant Contact Cons. . . . . 50 Times the Quarterly Goals
Sunday School Average . . . . Divide "Growth Goal" by 4

244

Chapter Eleven

New Convert Care

After grabbing a quick lunch, Elder Keller and Steve headed for the former's stately country home. An ice-cold rain fell once again in a steady, continuous drizzle, giving a somber appearance to the dreary, ashen sky. The wind had picked up, giving promise of a gathering storm. Fitful gusts threw waves of spray against the car as it splashed through sodden streets.

Within the auto, the two preachers sat quietly, wrapped in their own thoughts. Much had happened within the last few days, much to think about and ponder.

As they pulled into the tree-lined drive, the elderly pastor suddenly snapped his fingers and pulled the car up short.

"I forgot."

"Forgot what?"

"To see Mark and Debbie."

"Who are Mark and Debbie?"

"They're a young couple I brought to the Lord through a Bible study last year. Mark was hurt on the job Monday. I meant to go by and see him on the way home. They live about thirty minutes from here. Do you mind if I run out there for a while?"

"No, sir," Steve answered, his mouth twitching toward a smile, "but I think with your knee hurting like this, it would be better if we drove."

The old pastor rolled his eyes and moaned. "Lord, spare me his dumb jokes."

In a few moments they were headed back down the same highway toward town.

"How did you happen to meet this couple, Elder?" Steve asked.

"By referral. Mark's brother, Ron, received the Holy Ghost in Louisiana last year. He then witnessed to Mark and Debbie at a family reunion here in Ellisburg. Ron later called the church and asked us to visit. I went out to see them and set up a Bible study. They then came to a revival last February and both received the Holy Ghost. They've been in church about eight months and are doing great. A couple more months and we can remove them from the New Convert Care System."[1]

"New Convert Care System? You mentioned that before. What is it?"

"That's the subject I'd planned for this morning before you sidetracked me. Actually, your care ministry should be in operation *before* you launch the spiral program. It can raise your new convert retention to over sixty percent."

Instruction, Fellowship, and Involvement

"Sounds good, but how does it work?" Steve pressed.

"It's built around three basic principles taken from the second chapter of Acts. Luke recorded that after the three thousand were baptized—and three thousand is a bunch of converts—they continued steadfastly in three areas: instruction, fellowship and unity of involvement. I feel these are the key elements needed to establish new converts."

"Instruction, fellowship and involvement," Steve repeated aloud. "That makes sense. Yet doesn't a new convert receive those by coming to church? I mean, the preaching and teaching are instruction. Then they have fellowship before and after each service. And going to church three times a week certainly is a lot more involvement than most ever had."

"That's true, Steve, in a general sense. However, new converts have special needs that are poorly met in only normal services. That would be like saying that the food Mom fixes for the rest of the family is sufficient for her newborn child. Babies have needs that adults do not. If those needs are ignored, the child may suffer."

Steve pondered this for a moment. "Is that why some churches keep so few converts? They're not caring for them properly?"

"That's exactly right," Elder Keller said, his voice emphatic. "They don't do it intentionally, any more than mothers at the turn of the century intentionally neglected their newborn children. The infant death rate a hundred years ago was almost thirty percent: almost one-third of the babies born never lived to see their first birthday. Today, it's less than five percent. Many babies who would have died when I grew up are being saved today to live normal, healthy lives. The reason is better prenatal and postnatal care practices. We have learned to care for newborns better."

247

The old pastor brought the car to a stop at a traffic light and turned to look at Steve, his eyes reflecting deep emotion. "The same applies to the church. If we will take better care of our new converts, we will see more solid, established Christians. Their survival corresponds directly to the amount of attention they get. At Apostolic Tabernacle, our new convert retention is almost eighty percent."

Steve whistled softly. "You must have some program. What are you doing?"

"Well, when an individual is baptized or receives the Holy Ghost, we begin to work with them immediately. This is important, because I have observed that most new converts who backslide do so within the first month or two—many the very first week. When someone receives the Holy Ghost, an urgency grips me. I realize that brand-new Christians are much like a newborn baby—very weak, very hungry, and very dependent upon Mother. That baby cannot live for long on its own. If a mother abandons her newborn child, it will quickly die.

"For example, remember the major earthquake several years ago that hit Mexico City? Remember the hospital that collapsed on the maternity ward, and how that seven days after the earthquake they dug several newborn babies out of the rubble alive? The world cried, 'It's a miracle.' However the medical community answered, 'Not so.' The doctors went on to explain that nature—we would say God—has given newborn babies the ability to survive for a period of time with no care whatsoever. If abandoned, their body will simply go into a state similar to hibernation—breathing, heart rate, and body functions slow way down—and they can survive this way for about seven or eight days. But after that their natural resources will run out. Death quickly follows.

"Too often it looks as if the new convert is doing fine on his own. The truth is, he is only living off that initial conversion experience. The mother must wake up and realize that she has a responsibility to feed, care, and shelter her newborn. The Bible describes the church as the mother of us all. The church must understand that newborn Christians are also weak, hungry, and dependent. It is vital that we begin to care for them as soon as possible.

"Remember, too," he continued, "that the devil is going to do all he can to make them stumble and fall. So we don't dare let a new convert leave without putting something in his hands, both for strength and nourishment and to defend against Satan's attack. To this end, Tommy and I have personally trained six first-night counselors. One of these counselors spends about twenty minutes with each convert at the same service in which he is baptized or receives the Holy Ghost."

"What do the counselors do?" Steve asked.

A horn blared from behind, reminding them that the traffic light had turned green. Brother Keller turned the car left before answering. "They first fill out a short information card on the converts.[2] They then explain four simple topics to them. The first is their new life. We clarify what has just taken place and how it fits into the new birth. If they haven't been baptized, baptism is explained. If they haven't received the Holy Ghost, this experience is explained also. But mainly, we stress the new beginning that comes by being born again. That way we defeat a major tactic the devil uses against new converts: dragging up their past that's now under the blood.

"The second topic is the devil's attack. We warn them that Satan may use family or friends to condemn their decision to live for God. He will try to make them stumble and sin. He will try to tempt them back into their old way of life. We encourage them not to sin, but if they do stumble—and all babies stumble while learning to walk—to get back up, tell the Lord they're sorry, and promise never to do it again.

"The third subject is what I call the three basic nutrients for new converts: daily prayer, daily Bible reading, and consistent church attendance. We explain briefly how to pray, what to read in the Bible, and when church services are held. We also explain why these three practices are so critical. Few know how to pray or where to begin Bible reading, and they can't afford to wait until lesson five of the new converts class to learn. They need to start praying and reading Scripture the very next day. Before this time they may have gone to church once a year. They might now think once a week is enough. How will they know differently unless we tell them?

"The last topic is very simple, yet extremely important. We let them know that *we care.* Many new converts have no one to talk to when they confront spiritual problems. They feel they're imposing upon the pastor and his time. They are reluctant to talk about personal struggles and weaknesses. Someone needs to reassure them that they should not—and cannot—fight these battles alone, that they can call or come by any time. We give them the phone numbers of the pastor, assistant pastor, care director, and first-night counselor to ensure that someone will be available when needed. We must realize that a newborn baby is not like an adult. What to us would seem a minor inconvenience is a major spiritual battle to them. They must have highly personalized attention. Finally, we give them a new convert booklet and tape."

"Booklet and tape?"

"The booklet we buy from the Pentecostal Publishing House.[3] The tape is simply Tommy teaching a forty-minute Bible study called *The Successful Christian Life*. This is a more comprehensive study of the basics of Christian living. He taught this to the entire church several years ago, and we give a copy of this lesson to each convert."[4]

Steve frowned. "So you fill out an information card, teach those four subjects, and give them a booklet and tape. How do you do all that in twenty minutes?"

"The object isn't to give them a comprehensive study, son, but to reveal a few basic principles. The booklet and tape will explain these subjects more fully. All we are trying to do is spark their hunger so that they will want more."

Steve nodded slowly. He turned to stare solemnly out the window at the traffic splashing past. He was beginning to catch a revelation of an entirely new approach— at least new to him—of establishing new Christians. It was an approach that took nothing for granted, that realized the new convert's survival was dependent, to a large degree, upon the church, not just the new convert.

He jotted these points down in his notes. "All right, what comes next?"

"Well, the information card is given to Sister Duncan, our New Convert Care director. She is the real backbone of the whole system."

"What does she do?"

"My, so many things," he said, shaking his head. "That is why I require New Convert Care to be its own department. It's too big a responsibility and too important a job to put within another department. The first thing she will do is appoint what we call a care partner for the convert. This is almost always the person who brought the individual to the Lord—the spiritual parent. We stress to this person that, as a new parent, he or she has some basic responsibilities to this spiritual child the Lord has given."

"Responsibilities?"

"Sure. There are ten in all. We explain these in a letter sent to every care partner.[5] The most important is to help feed their children. We always ask the care partner to teach a ten- or twelve-week Bible study in the convert's home. We also enroll the convert in the new life class, which is taught at the church during Sunday school."

"Why both?" Steve wondered. "Isn't the home Bible study enough?"

"Well, the home Bible study is extremely important. Not only for the information given, but also for the bond of friendship that develops between the parent and child. This is irreplaceable. However, the new life class is *essential* to their survival. It will teach them the basics of Christian living that they desperately need at this early stage. That new convert must know quickly how to pray, fight the devil, overcome the flesh, and study the Word. Nor can they wait until you get around to preaching it. In fact, Steve, I feel that both are so critical, I make their completion a condition of church membership."

"You're kidding!"

"No, I couldn't be more serious. If we don't put some teeth into it, they won't realize the importance. Other denominations have been doing this for years with what they call catechism, and with good reason. If a proper foundation is not established at the beginning, then farther down the road a storm is going to blow them over. I have yet to lose a convert because of this requirement, and it has certainly paid off.

"The next essential key," he continued, "is fellowship. One way we cover this need is with dinner ministries."

The young man laughed. "Dinner ministries! Hey, I like it. I have some folks who are great at that already. In fact, I can't get them to put down the fork."

The old man smiled patiently. "Few people realize the importance of friends and fellowship to the new convert. The number of friends that the convert has will have a direct relationship upon his staying in church. I read one research report that compared fifty new members who were still active after six months with fifty new members who dropped out after six months. The converts that stayed had at least *seven* close friends in church. Those who dropped out had less than *two*. The final conclusion of the study was this: the number of friends new members make and how quickly they make them will directly influence whether they stay in church or not.[6]

"You see, Steve, friends are your support group. They are the ones who help you when you're down. They make you feel wanted, needed, and a part of the group. Since this is so important, I decided a few years ago that I wasn't going to leave it to chance. We began our dinner ministries program, and so far it's working great."

253

"How does it work? Do you simply invite the new convert over for dinner?"

"Exactly. You find this was a consistent pattern in the New Testament church. Luke said, 'They continued stedfastly in the apostles' doctrine and fellowship, and in breaking of bread. . . .' I don't feel it was an accident that so many important events in the life of Christ and in the Book of Acts occurred around a dinner table. There is something intimate about sitting down to a meal together, and it is by far the best way to make a friend. When a new convert eats with a church member and they spend the evening in fun and fellowship, that convert leaves having a close friend, not just a casual acquaintance. The New Convert Care director, after obtaining pastoral approval, assigns a different family each month to have the convert over for dinner. By the end of ten months, the convert has at least ten solid friends in church."

"The convert knows nothing about what's going on?" Steve interrupted.

"Correct. He simply feels that this is the friendliest, most outgoing church in town. The care director also plans a special social for all new converts and care partners each quarter. One time they'll have a potluck social, another quarter is a softball game and picnic. The third quarter might be an all night lock-in prayer meeting and breakfast, and then once each year I try to have all new converts over to my house for a barbecue."

"So not only do they develop friends with the church members, but also with one another!" Steve exclaimed.

"That's right. Now when they come to church they feel the bond of love and friendship. And the bond can be strengthened even more by the third key element: involvement. This is important for their own Christian development. A busy saint is usually a happy saint. The old cliche 'Use them or lose them' applies well here. An old concept in Pentecost used to be 'Sit for a year and prove yourself; after that we'll use you.' What that did was train new converts to do nothing. So after the year was up they did what they were taught to do—nothing. You see, Steve, the first year is the new convert's most impressionable time. Patterns and spiritual habits will be established that will remain with them from then on. As soon as the convert has stabilized somewhat—usually after a month or two—he needs to be involved in a church ministry. He can be used in an outreach ministry even sooner."

"Can't you hurt them by using them too soon?" Steve questioned.

"With some things, yes. The care director always works with the pastor to find a suitable place in the vineyard. I realize different people mature at different rates. Even so, everyone should be involved somewhere within four months. If not, then something is wrong. It would be like a baby who has never walked after two years."

"So," Steve injected, "Mother, meaning the church, should encourage her child to walk as soon as it's able, right?"

"Exactly. We have all our new converts fill out a talent form after two months. It asks about interests, hobbies, skills, and the like. We then talk with their care partners to get an idea of where the converts would enjoy working. We have even created a few special ministries specifically for new converts: the New Life Chorale, a new

255

convert's bus route, a new convert's maintenance crew, and so on. Of course, we also use new converts in all types of outreach: home Bible study assistant, bus worker, C.C.C., Sunday school teacher's aid, Saturday door knocking, and so on. In the church ministries, new converts work well in Ladies Auxiliary, the men's fellowship, youth ministries, maintenance, ushering and sometimes even in the choir or orchestra. But wherever they are involved, we always pair them with a mature saint as an instructor. We never turn the convert loose on his own."

"This sounds fantastic, Elder, but how do you keep track of it all? If you had twenty or thirty new converts, you would be running in circles trying to make sure everything is covered, especially if they are all in different stages of maturity."

"Well, that was a problem when we first started. However, we have now developed a simple report form that the New Convert Care director hands in each month. (See figure 15.) The care director spends two or three evenings on the phone each month to fill it out. As long as it's completed, then everything is covered. The pastor can glance down the report and quickly identify any converts who are struggling. The report shows everything from church attendance to dinner ministry assignments. This way we are able to solve problems before they get out of hand."

Steve nodded thoughtfully, chewing softly on the end of his pen. Finally he took a deep breath and let it out slowly, saying more to himself than the elder pastor, "When I think of all the converts we have lost in the last three years . . ." He shook his head. "If I had kept even half, we would be averaging over two hundred."

Brother Keller nodded without replying.

New Convert Care Confidential Report

8-7-89 Date

JULY 89 For The Month Of

New Convert's Name	Months In Your Care	H.G. & Baptism Date	New Life Class Attendance	Home Bible Study Attendance	Sunday Night Attendance	Mid-week Service Attendance	Care Partner's Name & Care Partner's Report	Dinner Ministries Assignment	Involvement Church & Outreach Min.	Any Problem's Or Needs?
Tom Bodden	10	10-28 11-1	Complete	Complete	5 out of 5	4 out of 5	John Elkins - Doing Very Good	Tom & Lisa Rodriguel	Ushers Home Bible Study	None
Debbie Bodden	10	10-28 11-1	Complete	Complete	4 out of 5	4 out of 5	Same ↑	Same ↑	Ladies Aux - Home Bible Study	None
Larry Cantu	10	10-5 10-5	Complete	Complete	5 out of 5	5 out of 5	James Bass - Needs More Friends	Mike McAlister	Bus Maintenance Street Services	None
Rick Mirror	9	11-13 11-19	4 out of 5	3 out of 5	3 out of 5	3 out of 5	Donnie & Rhonda Falwell - Doing All Right	John & Rea Thomas	Choir & Music V. Follow up	Needs Job
Nancy Mirror	9	11-16 11-19	4 out of 5	3 out of 5	3 out of 5	3 out of 5	Having Financial Problems	Same ↑	Choir V. Follow up	Might Need Food
Lisa Redondo	8	12-16 12-16	1 out of 5	None	1 out of 5	None	Tammy Allen - Doing Poor - Sugg. You Call	Tom & Ellen Rickles	Sunday School Deaf Min.	Having Trouble w/ Friends
Mitch Pietz	8	12-14 12-16	5 out of 5	4 out of 5	5 out of 5	5 out of 5	Allen Smith - Doing Very Good	Mark & Debbie Tracy	Maintenance Youth Min.	None
Theresa Pietz	8	12-15 12-16	5 out of 5	4 out of 5	5 out of 5	5 out of 5	Same ↑	Same ↑	Hostesses Youth Min.	None
Mike O'Conner	7	1-14 2-3	2 out of 5	1 out of 5	1 out of 5	None	Jack & Tammy Thomeius - Very Bad - Needs Help Now. Wont come to church (Mike)	Jerry & Ann Pekos	None Bus Ministry	(See me)
Ann O'Conner	7	1-14 2-3	5 out of 5	2 out of 5	5 out of 5	5 out of 5	Same ↑	Same ↑	Ladies Aux. Bus Ministry	(See me)

God Will Shut Up Her Womb

The old pastor slowed down and turned off the highway into a large group of modest custom homes. A thick brick wall and high colonnade stood sentry on both sides of the development entrance. The center marker announced in bold brass letters that they were entering The Bluffs and that new models were available.

"Mark and Debbie live just around the corner here," Elder Keller said. "I think you'll be surprised to see how far they have come in eight months. They are teaching a Bible study themselves now and have already brought several friends to the Lord."

They pulled up in front of an attractive ranch-style home, the small yard neat and well kept. A tricycle and a pair of toy boxing gloves, now soaked with rain, lay next to the porch, giving evidence that children lived there also. A new pickup sat in the driveway. Steve grinned when he saw the bumper stickers arranged boldly upon the tailgate. "Ask Me about Home Bible Studies" and "People of the Name . . . Jesus" were but two of many.

Upon hearing their knock, Debbie came to the door. She was short, petite, and in her mid thirties. Her long, blond hair was pulled back into a pony tail. She brightened with a smile as she saw them, pleased with the unexpected visit. After greeting and talking a moment, she led them through several large, well-decorated rooms to the back of the house. There they found Mark, propped up in bed with a strained back, surrounded by the evening newspaper.

Mark appeared older than his wife, maybe in his early forties. Where Debbie was short, Mark was tall with thick shoulders and large hands. His dark, leathery skin looked almost comical in the white and pink striped pajamas. His sharp, rugged face would have looked more comfortable behind the wheel of a heavy truck than in a sickbed. Thankfully he would not be there long. The doctor said he could return to work in a few days.

Brother Keller introduced Steve as they shook hands. All four sat and talked for a good hour drinking coffee and eating hot blueberry turnovers that Debbie had taken from the oven only moments before.

After praying with them and saying their good-byes, Brother Keller and Steve headed home for the second time that day. The young man sat silently, listening to the methodical slap of the windshield wipers and staring out the side window at the rain that still drizzled upon the countryside. Within his mind a question was forming, something to which he could find no answer.

"Elder, why is it that some churches have great revivals—sometimes two, three, even five hundred souls—and yet when you look back a year later only a handful are still living for God? To me, that seems to be such a waste. Why did God give them such a powerful revival when they had no capacity or program to contain it?"

The elder pastor glanced at Steve with a sad smile. "Well, son, I must admit I've wondered that myself. The only answer I can give you is that God will always honor His Word. Spiritual laws are much like the physical laws of nature. If you have the proper conditions present— good soil, ample moisture, quality seed, and plentiful sunshine—then the seed is going to grow. There is nothing that says the seed must have a barn built before it will produce. By the same token, a child will be born regardless

259

of whether the parents are ready to raise it, have food in the cupboard, have clothes to provide, or have a home for shelter. So if you plant the Word in hungry hearts, if those hearts are open to the Spirit of God, and if they surrender their lives to Jesus Christ, then new souls will be born into the kingdom. The law of sowing and reaping will always produce."

The old pastor paused to shrug his shoulders, then continued. "But what good is it to harvest grain if it rots in the field? Or to pick fruit and let it spoil? I feel this grieves the heart of God. Too often we say, 'All right God, after you send the harvest, I'll build the barn,' but by then it's too late. While the barn is being built most of the harvest will perish. Son, remember this: God is not in the business of making backsliders. God wants your church to be ready to handle a hundred-soul revival before He gives you one. One hundred souls are one hundred babies. Someone must take care of them, befriend them, counsel them, and train them. So an effective new convert care system must be your *highest* priority, even before you launch your spiral ministry. We must not neglect the fruit that the Lord gives us. To do so is to grieve the Lord of the harvest."

Key Concept Twelve

Thou shalt not neglect thy newborn children, for they are the fruit of thy labor.

Steve leaned his head back, his voice matter-of-fact as he stared at the light cream headliner of the car. "I read a newspaper story a few months back about a mother who left her five young children at home alone without any supervision. The neighbors later said she did this quite often. One night her little boy started playing with matches and caught the house on fire—Momma wasn't home. Four of her children died in the flames. The courts charged the mother with third-degree murder—child abuse by neglect."

He raised his head to glance over at the old pastor. "So is that what you're saying, Elder? That the church is guilty of spiritual child abuse if it neglects new converts?"

The elderly pastor nodded. "I'm not saying it, son, I think the Lord is saying it. A few years ago the Lord gave a vision to one of our ministers up north. In the vision he saw an old brick hospital with large concrete steps. A doctor came out of the front doors carrying a newborn child in his arms. A nurse walked alongside, smiling and looking on. 'Isn't it wonderful!' he heard them exclaim. 'Another new baby!' They then put the child on the hospital steps and went home rejoicing. He saw this happen again and again until dozens of newborn babies lay upon the steps, all dying because of neglect. The Lord then spoke to the minister and said, 'That is exactly what is happening in My church!'[7] Steve, I personally feel that if such a condition persisted in a church, God would eventually shut up her womb until the problem was solved."

The old pastor was looking at the young man, his eyes mirroring the depth of his heart-rending emotion. Perhaps the old gentleman was so caught up in their conversation that he wasn't watching the road properly. More than likely, though, even if he had been looking straight ahead, he wouldn't have had time to stop. As they rounded a wide, tree-lined curve, three large cows stood in the middle of the road.

"Look out!" Steve cried.

The old pastor swerved right and slammed on the brakes, throwing the large, old car into a wild spin on the wet asphalt surface. The last thing Steve remembered seeing was the trees rushing toward them as the car careened out of control.

Chapter Twelve

"It's Up to You Now"

The ambulance slowly pulled away from the wide emergency-room entrance at the same moment that Tommy Keller drove up. Still rolling, he jammed the shift lever impatiently into park, causing the large car to lurch to a jarring stop. Leaping out, he ran toward the sliding double doors and in his haste nearly knocked over Steve, who was on his way out.

"Steve! Thank God you're all right! How's Dad?" His face was a frozen mask, but his eyes and voice were sheathed in fear.

"Hold it—take it easy," Steve said quietly. "He's fine. They have him in the examining room now. He received a nasty knock on his head and may have broken a rib, yet it's nothing really serious. The doctor said a few stitches on his forehead and the bleeding should stop."

"Are you sure? Where is he? Is his heart all right? When can I see him?" Like lawyer to defendant, Tommy fired questions one after the other as he followed Steve back into the busy waiting room.

Steve held up his hand to calm him. "In a few minutes.

263

The doctor went in to see him about ten minutes ago. He should be through any time. However, the head nurse wanted to talk to you. She'll be back in a—no, here she comes now."

A stout, middle-aged woman dressed in plain hospital whites walked briskly into the waiting room, a large clipboard grasped in one hand and a pen clutched in the other. "Reverend Keller? You're Jeremiah Keller's son?" She spoke without a smile, her tone crisp and formal.

Tommy frowned as he nodded.

"If you don't mind, we need to get some information about your father. Could you come with me?"

As she led Tommy quickly away, Steve found an empty seat and sank down in exhaustion. He glanced at his watch. Only forty-five minutes had passed since the accident, but it seemed like hours. So much had happened in such blinding rapidity. He closed his eyes, his strength totally spent. In jumbled disarray, as if he were viewing so many unfocused snapshots from a dime-store camera, his mind played back a hazy panorama following the crash of metal and glass.

The car came to a wrenching halt against several massive trees, the front end angling sharply downward into a muddy, rain-swollen watercourse. Steve was wearing his seat belt, so the jarring stop did little more than throw him violently forward, though his hand was bruised as it slammed into the dash upon impact.

Elder Keller was less fortunate. With no seat belt to restrain him, the old pastor was forcibly lifted from his seat and hurled forward, which caused his chest to strike the top edge of the steering wheel painfully and his head to snap sharply upward into the already shattered wind-

264

shield. With a strangled groan he slumped over in the seat.

Steve sat dazed for several moments, the icy rain splattering upon the shattered, broken glass. Only after Brother Keller moaned softly a second time did he grasp hold of himself. Fumbling to release his seat belt, he turned his attention to the one beside him. Finding a weak pulse, he applied his handkerchief to the old man's bleeding forehead, and after a moment the flow greatly lessened. He then kicked the door open and staggered into the puddled roadway to wave down an approaching car. After a quick word, the driver sped away to the next house to call for help.

Ten minutes later, two husky attendants loaded Brother Keller and Steve into the flashing white van and raced toward the hospital, the siren screaming an urgent cry. Steve remembered little of the ride there, only the sick, nauseating fear he felt for an old man of God he had grown to love dearly.

It was Tommy's commanding tone that shoved the somber images aside and pulled him back to the present. The pastor stood over him, shaking his shoulder. "Come on. Dad's out of emergency. The doctor said we could see him if we hurried."

They walked quickly down a long, polished corridor and into an examining room that smelled strongly of anti-septic. Elder Keller lay motionless on a white-sheeted bed with the back propped up, an IV inserted into one arm and a wide bandage around his head.

He smiled weakly as they came in. "It's about time. I began to think you'd gone to make funeral arrangements."

Tommy grasped his father's hand tightly. "How do you feel, Dad?"

"Sort of foolish," he mumbled weakly. "Those ol' cows surprised me. I should have known better than try to swerve on that wet road."

"Well, thank the Lord you're all right," Tommy replied with conviction. "I just talked to the doctor. You should be out in no time."

"They're going to let me go now, aren't they?"

"No, Dad . . . the doctor is afraid of that big bruise on your chest. Nothing's broken, but the trauma may be dangerous to your heart. They're going to hold you overnight for observation."

The old pastor sighed. "I never have liked hospitals. Every magazine in the place is six months old."

Tommy glanced sideways at Steve. They both chuckled.

Tommy's wife and several others came in a moment later. Everyone stayed into the early evening, until Elder Keller was settled in a private room. The doctor examined him once again, then stepped into the hall to talk privately with Tommy. Soon after, the doctor recommended that everyone go home and let his patient rest.

Against his father's protest, Tommy decided to spend the night at the hospital. He said he wanted to keep Elder Keller company, but Steve detected a worried note in his voice. Before leaving he called Tommy aside.

"Is something wrong?"

"Why?"

"The doctor didn't look too happy."

"Well, it may not be serious, but the x-rays show some swelling around his heart. As weak as his heart is, they

266

fear what the stress might cause. It's possible for him to have another heart attack. If the pressure doesn't go down by morning, they want to put him in the intensive care unit. We need to pray."

Steve nodded. "You want me to stay with you?"

"No, you've had a bad shake-up yourself. Go home and rest. With the Lord's help, everything will be fine in the morning."

Steve squeezed his friend's shoulder. "I'll be praying."

Steve drove Tommy's car to Elder Keller's home. Although Lazarus met him at the door with a soft whine and questioning bark, the large house felt dark and cheerless, the warmth and light from the wide hearth having long since died. Steve knelt down to scratch his short-legged friend. He looked into the dog's deep brown eyes, and feeling somewhat foolish, explained what had happened. He hoped the sound of his voice, rather than his words, would comfort the old hound. He couldn't help but wonder what would happen to the old dog should Brother Keller die. He shrugged off the thought.

After feeding the dog, Steve fixed a sandwich for himself. He then tried to read but found he couldn't concentrate. His chest hurt and his neck was stiff. He prayed for a while, then finally fell into a restless sleep upon the living-room sofa, his Bible lying open beside him.

Four Distinct Stages

He didn't wake until midmorning. The rain had stopped, and a cheerful sun had burned away the clouds, bringing songbirds to full voice in the trees outside. Quickly, not even bothering to change clothes, he washed and shaved, then headed back into town.

267

As he stepped into the hospital room he was pleased and surprised to find Elder Keller sitting up in bed, a large tray of food before him. The IV stand beside the bed had been replaced with the soft, chirping voice of an electronic heart monitor. The ill-appearing, full head wrap was not but a medium square of gauze bandage. When the old pastor greeted him, his voice was rich and strong.

"Morning! Pull up a chair and have some breakfast."

"Hey," Steve exclaimed, "you're looking better! How do you feel?"

"Oh, fair to middlin', but a sight better than last night. And guess what? For some reason, my knee stopped hurting. Weather must have cleared up."

Steve grinned with relief. "I'm not so worried about your knee, Elder. What's the doctor say about your heart?"

"Ah!" the old pastor growled, waving his hand in mock disgust. He took a bit of toast. "What do they know? My ticker will keep on ticking until the Lord wants it to stop." He paused as if to consider what he had just said. Then he shrugged. "However, the doctor was here this morning. He said I'm looking good."

Suddenly Steve felt much better. He glanced around. "Where's Tommy?"

"He went to the cafeteria to get some coffee. He looks worse than I do. Don't think he slept much. He should be back soon."

The young man eased himself down on the foot of the bed. The elder pastor did look better. The ruddy color was back in his face, and his eyes no longer carried dark circles beneath but instead held the usual warm, laughing look. The steady, rhythmical chirrup from the heart monitor seemed to give further testimony of his improved condition.

"Boy, Elder," Steve said after a moment's silence, "you had me worried yesterday. When they pulled you out of the car your face was as gray as death. In fact, I thought we had lost you."

The old pastor flashed a toothy smile. "You kidding? And let you off the hook? I haven't worked with you all this week to let you walk away and do as you please like a fox with feathers in his teeth. You need someone to check on you, son—someone to make sure you do something with what you've learned. Remember what I told you? People don't do what you expect, they do what you inspect—and I'm your self-appointed inspector. I'll be calling you every month for the next year to see how you're following through with this material."

The young man laughed, then leaned back on his elbow with a sigh. "This week has been incredible, Elder. I glanced through my notebook this morning after prayer. It's bulging. I have so much I want to do, I don't know where to start."

The old pastor nodded. "I know you don't. What you need now is a schedule of implementation. You know what I mean? A plan of action to follow step by step. You see, son, if you're not careful, you'll fall into the same trap of trying to do too much too quickly, just like your directors after an annual planning retreat. If you get too much going at once, your entire program will collapse."

The young man scratched his head in dismay. "That makes sense, sir, but how do I know what to do first? I need to do everything you've shown me, and it needed to be done last year."

"Hmm," Brother Keller mused aloud, "Let's see . . . you have your notebook with you? No?" He glanced quickly around the room. Then with one bony finger he pointed. "There, use that clipboard and paper hanging on the end of my bed."

"No way!"

"What do you mean no way?"

"That's your medical chart!"

"They can make a new one."

"But . . ."

"Don't argue with me, son! Who do you think's paying the bills here, anyway? Turn that paper over and write on the back."

Shaking his head with amusement, Steve obeyed.

"Okay," Brother Keller continued, "The first thing you need to do . . ." and for the next ten minutes, the old pastor kept up a running commentary, detailing when each phase of the growth program should be launched.[1]

When he finished, Steve laid his pencil down and stood up to stretch. "My, Elder," he said with a yawn, "when you look at everything all at once, it's enough to bury you. But outlined like this, it sounds simple."

"Any goal or project, son, when broken into a step-by-step plan, will be easier. But don't let that deceive you into thinking that everything will go satin smooth. It won't. In fact, you can expect this to be one of the most difficult projects you'll ever undertake."

"What do you mean?" the younger pastor responded with surprise.

"Steve, I'm sure you realize that with any new material there is a learning process to go through. The first three or four months will be difficult. Problems are

270

inevitable, especially with a completely new management structure. In working with other pastors, I've observed four distinct stages in implementing this material.''

"Which are?"

"Which are these," Elder Keller replied. "The first stage is *confusion* and will begin immediately following your retreat. This is the learning stage. Although your leaders may understand the material, this will be their first attempt in actually doing it. The first time you try anything new is always a struggle. The trick is to tackle only one problem at a time. You may have to work hand in hand with some of your outreach and department directors until they grasp how you want things to work. Your emphasis in this stage should be upon training. Give them an exact pattern to follow.

"The second stage is *communication.* After two or three months of apparent chaos, your directors will begin to understand better what you are trying to do. They'll start giving you feedback on what does and does not work. Remember, just because something isn't working is no cause to throw it away. Fix it. It may only need a bit of adjustment to fit your situation better. Place your emphasis here upon creativity adapting the program to produce the results you want.

"The third stage is *cooperation.* Here is where everything begins to flow more smoothly and you begin to see results. However, it's been a long hard pull to get here—usually six to eight months. But finally the resisters stop resisting, your outreaches start producing, and your new converts stick. It's almost downhill from here.

"The last stage begins after you've used the entire program for almost a year. You have custom-designed

271

everything to fit, and most of the bugs have been worked out. Now your leaders will develop *commitment.* You'll know you've reached it when you hear them say things like 'Now we're really moving' and 'This is the only way to go.' The longer you use it, the better it gets."

The Cost of Pentecost

"I'm glad you told me this, Elder," Steve said. "I guess I expected everything to click along right from the start."

"Most men do. That's a real problem I've had in the past. They don't realize it starts out slow and builds up speed, like the law of inertia. Ever study physics?"

"Uh . . ." Steve scratched his head. "It's been a long time. That's one of the laws of motion, isn't it?"

"Right. The law of inertia is that an object at rest has a desire and tendency to remain at rest, and an object in motion has a desire and tendency to remain in motion. Case in point—ever try to stop a freight train? That's an object in motion that desires to stay in motion. Yet the opposite holds true too. If a freight train is standing still, it sometimes takes four locomotives at full power just to get it rolling. Tremendous energy is required. Slowly the train will begin to move, then faster and faster, until it reaches peak speed and momentum takes over. Then, one engine after another can shut down, until one engine alone can maintain the desired speed.

"What I'm saying is this, Steve: your church is now an object at rest. To get your church in motion is going to take a tremendous amount of time and effort. You must realize this and be willing to pay the price. You have probably heard it said that there is a cost to having a

272

Pentecost. For you, *cost* simply means *commitment*. The true meaning of the word *commitment* is to be willing to give up something in order to gain something greater. It's the kind of attitude that says 'If I perish, I perish.'

"Hundreds of years ago, Machiavelli, the famous Italian politican, wrote, 'There is nothing more difficult to carry out, nor more doubtful of success, nor more dangerous to handle, than to begin a new order of things.'[2] Psychologists will tell you that one of people's greatest fears is change. They resist it. However, any pastor that is successful must be willing to accept that risk. This means being willing to try something new. As the old saying goes, 'A turtle gets nowhere until he sticks his neck out.'"

"But," Steve said with a grin, "what if I stick my neck out, and somebody cuts it off? What I mean is, what if this program doesn't work for me as it does for you?"

"So what if it doesn't? Is what you're doing now working? You must be willing to fail at times if you ever expect to succeed. I'm not saying it will fail, but there's a certain amount of risk involved in anything new.

"In the Parable of the Talents, the two faithful servants risked their master's money by investing it. The third was condemned because he took no risk. You must be willing to take a chance, too. No pastor will fight his way to consistent growth without exercising the fullest measure of faith, courage, determination, and resolution. The man who gets somewhere does so because he has first resolved in his own mind that this direction is the will of God. Then he has enough stick-to-it-iveness to transform God's will into reality.[3] Solomon put it best when he said, 'If thou faint in the day of adversity, thy strength is small.'"

Steve slowly nodded, his gaze upon the clipboard before him. In his hand lay the plan of action he was now determined to follow. The old pastor gave a tired sigh and lay back on his pillow, also lost in thought. He knew he had done all he could; it was now out of his hands.

It was into this solemn atmosphere that Tommy walked a moment later. He glanced from one to the other. "Hey, why so serious? You look like the Apostle Peter the day before Easter."

Steve smiled wanly. "Your dad just dropped a bomb on me. I guess I didn't realize how much work was going to be involved in putting these plans into effect. However, with the Lord's help, I'm going to do it. I'm absolutely convinced this is what my church needs."

Tommy grinned mischievously. "I'll tell you the secret, Steve, to making Dad's system work. All you need to do is work half days."

"Half days?"

"Sure, and you can even choose which twelve-hour part suits you best!" Steve groaned as Tommy chuckled at his own wit.

"Has the doctor come back with the test results?" Tommy asked.

"He stuck his head in just after you left," his father replied. "He said the results would be back this afternoon. If they are passable I can go home."

Tommy nodded as he yawned widely. "In that case, I'm going to let Steve keep you company while I get some rest. That chair makes a lousy bed. I woke up every half hour." He glanced at his watch. "I'll be back around one o'clock to take you to our house. You'll be staying with us, Dad, until you're completely recovered. No arguing!"

274

Tommy hugged his father and had a quick word of prayer before leaving.

Brother Keller and Steve talked for a while longer until the old pastor began to tire. Steve was surprised to find how weary he felt also. He closed the blinds and drew the heavy, woven drapes across the window, bringing the room into near darkness. In a few moments both men slipped softly to sleep.

As Steve slept, he dreamed. He dreamed he was back at Brother Keller's home. The house was cold and pallid, even more so than the night before. His steps echoed strangely in the almost empty rooms. Much of the furniture was gone; only an occasional item remained, looking forlorn and abandoned and covered with a thin layer of dust. He looked for the old pastor, calling his name repeatedly. The sound of his voice seemed harsh in the stillness. He felt no fear but rather an uneasy loneliness.

At his heels, Lazarus whined softly. Occasionally the old dog would bark, as if he too were calling for someone. Finally the old dog sat back on his haunches and pointed his nose in the air. He howled a long, thin cry. Steve was puzzled as he listened to the dog. The strange, high-pitched wail seemed to go on and on . . .

The heavy door flew open with a crash, jerking Steve awake. Two nurses rushed past him to the bedside of the old man. With a horrible, sick feeling, Steve realized the high-pitched cry was the alarm on the heart monitor above Brother Keller's bed.

A doctor pushed past the nurses and began manual heart massage, shouting out orders to first one nurse then the other. Steve watched the fevered activity in a dazed horror, a knot forming deep in his chest and stomach.

Over and over he heard himself whisper, "Jesus . . . Jesus . . ." He later remembered wondering if this was still a part of the dream.

It's Up to You Now

Tommy came down the hospital corridor at a dead run, dodging around one person after another, slowing only as he rounded the hall corner to the room. The two nurses were just wheeling the cardioresuscitator out of the room. The doctor met him coming out the door, his mouth set in a tight line, his eyes grave.

"Reverend, I'm sorry. There's little we can do. He's had a massive myocardial infarction—simply put, a major heart attack. We have the heart muscle functioning again, but it's extremely weak. The damage done is irreparable. He's semiconscious, yet he may not know you're there. He's slowly going comatose as his blood pressure drops. I wish we could do something, but at his age . . ." The doctor put his hand on Tommy's shoulder and shook his head. Tommy hurried into the room.

The drapes were still drawn, the room lights darkened. Steve had his chair pulled up beside the bed, the old pastor's hand clutched in his own. His head was bowed as if in prayer. He looked up as Tommy came in, his eyes swollen and wet.

Neither said a word. Tommy moved to the other side of the bed and gazed into the age-worn face. His father's eyes were sunken, his cheeks drawn and thin. Beads of perspiration shimmered upon his flush, pale forehead. To Tommy, he looked as if he had aged ten years in just a few hours. He picked up the limp, wrinkled hand and leaned over the bed.

"Dad . . . Dad?" his voice broke, quivering with emotion. "Can you hear me, Dad?"

The old man's eyes fluttered faintly and opened, yet still vacant and unfocused. "Tommy . . . I . . . hear you, boy." The old pastor's breath was faint and shallow, his voice barely a whisper.

"Don't talk, Dad, save your strength. You'll . . . you're going to be all right. We . . . Steve and I . . . we're going to pray. God's going to heal you. Just hang on, Dad." Tommy's tone was tight and filled with desperation.

The old pastor closed his eyes slowly, almost as if he didn't hear. But, then, after a moment he murmured softly, as if to himself, "No . . . no, son, not this time." As Tommy began to reply, Brother Keller interrupted him, his voice coming somewhat stronger. "No . . . let me talk. I have something to say . . . not much time . . . to say it."

Tommy broke and began to weep. Tears flowed from the old man's eyes also.

"Son, you're the only child your mother and I had. We've always been close," the old pastor paused, his thin, sallow lips trembling slightly. "I've been proud of you, son. You're everything I ever wanted you to be. I . . . love you so much . . ."

His voice trailed off, his breath coming in short, quick gasps, marking time with the heart monitor above his bed. What he couldn't say with his voice, his eyes revealed. Tommy leaned over and embraced his father, sobbing. They clung together for several seconds, until slowly the old man's arm slipped from around his son's neck and fell loosely upon the bed. The heart monitor continued to beep out a dull, somewhat irregular beat.

Steve was standing now, crying unashamedly and gazing at the old man of God whose life was slowly draining away before him—a fellow warrior of the Cross, one who had fought a good fight, finished the course, and kept the faith.

But why did it have to end now? There was still so much good the elderly pastor could do. So much knowledge and experience. Where was God now? Why did not God raise him up? Why should it end here? What purpose could his death serve?

As if to answer, slowly, softly, a calm swept into the room and into their hearts. Soft chill bumps passed over Steve's back and neck. Steve glanced at Tommy, who looked up at the same moment. He felt it too.

Unexpectedly, Elder Keller opened his eyes a second time. His look was glazed, yet a glimmer of the old spark remained. As his eyes came into focus they rested upon Steve. The old man smiled faintly.

"Well, Steve," he whispered, "it's up to you now . . . did all I could. I . . . didn't quite make it, did I?"

As the old pastor paused, Steve wondered what he meant. "Didn't make what, sir?" he asked. When Brother Keller didn't reply, Steve thought he hadn't heard. He was about to repeat the question when the old man continued.

"Fifty . . . I . . . I didn't teach fifty . . . so wanted to . . . no time now." Elder Keller slowly closed his eyes again.

Steve thought he had drifted off once more, but he soon looked up. "I only had thirteen more to go . . ." He blinked his eyes several times, and his gaze suddenly became sharp and clear. His look bore into the young pastor's soul.

"You!" his voice rasped, strangled yet clear. "You teach them. You can do it. I'm . . . I'm counting on you, boy! Don't let this die . . . with me!"

The old man stopped, his fervid gaze a piercing, narrow beam. He slowly reached up and gripped Steve's wrist with surprising strength, his voice now clear and strong.

"Go . . . teach the others . . . just as I have taught you!"

As if in a trance, Steve nodded his head.

The Essence of Knowledge

Years later, Steve would recall that precise moment, like a vibrant invocation reaching across the boundless destiny of time. He could still feel the power, the stirring, the quickening pull of the Spirit within. Each time the memory would grip him afresh—more like the voice of God than the voice of a man. It went beyond a simple request or even a commandment. It became a calling.

Although Jeremiah Keller calmly slipped into a coma and at 4:16 A.M., November 9, passed from this life into the next, a lifetime of practical experience lived in the heart of Pastor Steve Martin. Little did Steve realize what impact that one week would have, not only on his own ministry, but upon the ministries of hundreds of others. Men who were much like Steve Martin. Men who were urgently praying for answers. Men who were desperate for growth and revival. Men who were willing to do whatever it took to reach their cities with truth.

Pastor Martin did more than learn the principles; he used them. He adapted them and applied them one by one. He knew this was not everything, yet it was a start.

His church did not grow overnight, but like a tree planted by the water, it steadily flourished. The instructions of Elder Keller gave Steve the proper foundation. It aimed him in the right direction. He wrapped each truth with prayer and immersed it in both faith and sweat.

Elder Jeremiah Keller's prediction that Steve would reach his five-year goal much sooner held true: he reached it in three. The five-year mark found Pastor Martin's church averaging well over four hundred.

Today, twice that many years have passed. The church in Springville averages about eight hundred. A large fleet of eleven buses covers the expanding city, bringing both children and adults to the large house of God. The church employs two men to assist Brother Martin full time, not counting the Christian school staff. An evening Bible institute is forming out of the expanding leadership development classes. Many young men have gone out to establish growing churches because of Pastor Martin's faith in the mother-church concept. Elder Keller's advice has served him well.

A wise man once said, "The essence of knowledge is, once having it, to use it." So with this simple morsel of wisdom, this story comes to a close. The knowledge is yours; in the words of Jeremiah Keller, "It's up to you now."

Appendix

Key Concept Evaluation

The purpose of this appendix is to focus upon the twelve key principles presented in *Let My People Grow.* Too often today we find ourselves majoring on minors. Somehow, we must brush aside the trivial and bring back what is truly important. These twelve keys are not by any means everything we need to promote growth, but they are some of the most critical. They are applicable to churches of any size and in any situation.

Where exactly is your church? How do you stand as far as the basics are concerned? What are your prospects for growth? What areas need your greatest attention? The accompanying questionnaire may enlighten or even surprise you. Complete it as accurately as possible. There are five questions on each of the twelve key concepts. Each question allows you to respond on a one-to-five scale. Choose the number along the scale that best represents you and your church. Only rarely will you find yourself as a one or a five; most will fall somewhere in between. Add up your score after each set, place these totals at the end of the questionnaire, and determine your average.

The purpose of this evaluation is to reveal your weak areas. No church is strong in all areas. Some pastors are natural organizers; others are dreamers who possess great faith and vision. Still others are promoters and motivators, and some have a special spiritual sensitivity. You should capitalize upon your areas of strength and ability, using them to their greatest advantage. However, this does not mean you should totally forsake your weaknesses. If you know where you are weak, then you can put extra effort into those areas to strengthen them.

Abundant material is provided in the two-binder set *Total Church Growth* to help you do exactly that. It focuses upon each key concept and provides a wealth of suggestions, ideas, solutions to common problems, and effective outreach methods in an easy-to-understand format. The binder is designed to accompany and complement *Let My People Grow* and it includes six cassette tapes. It is available from either the Pentecostal Publishing House or the General Home Missions Division, 8855 Dunn Road, Hazelwood, MO 63042-2299, for $69.95.

As Abraham Lincoln so ably put it, "If we could first know where we are, and whither we are tending, we could better judge what to do and how to do it."

KEY CONCEPT ONE

Thou shalt have unshakable faith that thy church will grow, for this is God's plan and purpose for His church.

1. I would describe my attitude toward pastoring my church as

   ready to quit   extremely excited
          1-----2-----3-----4-----5

2. My desire for growth and my willingness to pay the price to have it are

   uncertain/unsure   burning/fervent
          1-----2-----3-----4-----5

3. I believe it is God's will for me to pastor a church that is (by my standards)

   small   large
          1-----2-----3-----4-----5

4. My current plans for future growth are

   non existent   fully developed
          1-----2-----3-----4----5

5. I feel that the potential for my church to at least double in the next three to five years is

   poor   fantastic
          1-----2-----3-----4----5

Total_____

283

Let My People Grow

KEY CONCEPT TWO

Thou shalt not wander aimlessly but shalt have positive direction, clear purpose, and definite goals.

1. My current understanding of how to set goals effectively and see them carried out is

  very limited   highly developed
  1----2----3----4----5

2. My use of goal setting in the past (in the church or personally) has been

  very limited   very extensive
  1----2----3----4----5

3. The goals I have set in the past have usually been

  unrealistically high or low   right on target
  1----2----3----4----5

4. My goals and plans for my church for the next *five years* are

  very vague and   well developed
  in my mind only   and in writing
  1----2----3----4----5

5. My goals and plans for my church *this* year are

  very vague and   well developed
  in my mind only   and in writing
  1----2----3----4----5

Total_____

KEY CONCEPT THREE

Thou shalt have unfailing faith in thy people, for they are laborers together with thee in God's vineyard.

1. I would *currently* describe my church as

an organizational nightmare				very well organized

1----2----3----4----5

2. Most of the routine tasks in my church I

do myself				delegate to others

1----2----3----4----5

3. I have organized my church into departments and drawn up an organizational chart

never or very long ago				in the past two years

1----2----3----4----5

4. Writing job descriptions for my church leaders is something that I

have never done before				have done—I have a complete, up-to-date set

1----2----3----4----5

5. New programs, ministries, and positions that I launch in my church usually

fall apart after a time				operate well

1----2----3----4----5

Total_____

KEY CONCEPT FOUR

Thou shalt inspire thy people to labor in harmony, dream in unity, and think creatively.

1. On the whole, I would describe the spirit of my department heads as

    dead and unmotivated — excited and highly motivated

    1----2----3----4----5

2. The percentage of departments that are doing poorly (not performing their duties well) is

    almost all of them (95%) — almost none of them (5%)

    1----2----3----4----5

3. My departments and department heads tend to

    work poorly together — work well together

    1----2----3----4----5

4. The last time I met individually with my department heads and discussed their department goals and problems was

    long ago, if ever — in the last twelve months

    1----2----3----4----5

5. The last time I met with all my department heads together to plan the coming year was

    long ago if ever — within the last twelve months

    1----2----3----4----5

Total_____

KEY CONCEPT FIVE

Thou shalt plan thy work effectively, keeping in mind thy ultimate aim and purpose.

1. I have trained my department heads in the concepts and values of planning and goal setting

    never   recently
    1----2----3----4----5

2. I ask my department heads to hand in a written outline of their plans

    never   each year
    1----2----3----4----5

3. I require most of my department heads to set number goals or quality improvement goals

    never   each year
    1----2----3----4----5

4. I evaluate all of my departments' progress toward reaching their goals

    seldom,   on a regular
    if ever   basis
    1----2----3----4----5

5. The plans of my various departments

    continually   seldom, if ever
    butt heads   conflict
    1----2----3----4----5

Total_____

Let My People Grow

KEY CONCEPT SIX

*Thou shalt not abandon thy people as they pursue their goals
but shall meet with them consistently to plan
in unity of purpose.*

1. I meet for at least one hour with all of my department
heads as a group for planning purposes
       seldom, if ever   weekly
              1-----2-----3-----4-----5

2. My departmental planning sessions are scheduled
       only when I feel   on a consistent,
       a need for one   regular basis
              1-----2-----3-----4-----5

3. The planning sessions that I call are
       poorly   very well
       attended   attended
              1-----2-----3-----4-----5

4. At our department planning sessions we
       get very   get a whole
       little done   lot done
              1-----2-----3-----4-----5

5. I would describe my departments as
       small, independent   a unified
       kingdoms   team
              1-----2-----3-----4-----5

              Total_____

288

KEY CONCEPT SEVEN

Thou shalt require thy people to give an account of their labors that they be not slothful in their duties and position.

1. Communication between my departments and me is
    very poor   very good
    1-----2-----3-----4-----5

2. I require most departments to hand in a written report
    rarely, if ever   at least monthly
    1-----2-----3-----4-----5

3. For the most part my departments are
    very negligent   very faithful in
    in their duties   their duties
    1-----2-----3-----4-----5

4. When asking a director to do a task I
    almost never check   almost always
    back with him   check back
    1-----2-----3-----4-----5

5. Procrastination among my leaders is
    a very big   no problem
    problem   at all
    1-----2-----3-----4-----5

Total_____

KEY CONCEPT EIGHT

Thou shalt impart wisdom and knowledge to thy people that they may grow and prosper in their calling.

1. The potential for good leadership among my current membership is

   terrible   excellent

   1-----2-----3-----4-----5

2. The current leadership in my church

   leaves a lot to   is proficient and
   be desired   well trained

   1-----2-----3-----4-----5

3. I have leadership development classes

   rarely, if ever   at least monthly

   1-----2-----3-----4-----5

4. My leadership training, when I have it, is

   only for a   for all who wish
   selected few   to work for God

   1-----2-----3-----4-----5

5. I express my appreciation to my church leadership

   rarely or never—I   often and in many
   I don't want them to   different ways
   get the big head

   1-----2-----3-----4-----5

Total_____

KEY CONCEPT NINE

Thou shalt call thy people continually to prayer, preaching, and praise, for therewith shall many souls be born into the kingdom.

1. In my church, before-service prayer is

something few
participate in

something almost
all participate in

1-----2-----3-----4-----5

2. Among my leadership, going to the prayer room before service is

an option that few
take advantage of

a requirement that
most participate in

1-----2-----3-----4-----5

3. In my church, I would describe the worship service, for the most part, as

quiet, passive
sedate

explosive, exciting,
powerful

1-----2-----3-----4-----5

4. The response of the congregation to the preaching, on the average is

Silence—you can
hear a pin drop

enthusiastic,
eager, vocal

1------2------3------4------5

5. In my church, the operation of the nine gifts of the Spirit are

rarely emphasized
and seldom seen

often evident and
strongly encouraged

1------2------3------4------5

Total_____

KEY CONCEPT TEN

Thou shalt inspire My people to sow My Word continually according to the pattern I have given thee within the Book.

1. The percentage of my people who are *actively* involved in some type of organized outreach is

   less than 5%   over 70%

   1------2------3------4------5

2. I personally stress to my congregation that their own involvement in soul winning is

   only an option; they   an integral part of
   can take it or leave   Christian living
   it

   1-----2-----3-----4-----5

3. I would describe our visitor follow-up program as

   zilch—don't   a full program:
   have one   letter, phone, visit,
                                 mailing list.

   1-----2-----3-----4-----5

4. The home Bible study ministry in my church is

   struggling at best;   active and well
   few, if any, are   participated in
   going

   1-----2-----3-----4-----5

5. My Sunday school program is best described as

   an educational program   a powerful, productive
   for saints' children only   outreach ministry

   1-----2-----3-----4-----5

Total_____

KEY CONCEPT ELEVEN

Thou shalt illustrate to thy people the ways of a soul winner, leading them diligently to win the lost.

1. Personal soul winning is something that I

seldom have time to do anymore

make time for each week

1-----2-----3-----4-----5

2. In the past twelve months, I have personally brought

nobody to salvation

over five souls to salvation

1-----2-----3-----4-----5

3. My own personal participation in teaching home Bible studies is

something I don't have time for

regular and consistent

1-----2-----3-----4-----5

4. The average number of visits I make to sinners each week to try and win them to God is

less than two

more than seven

1-----2-----3-----4-----5

5. When my people gather for various outreach activities

I am rarely, if ever, present

I am almost always present

1-----2-----3-----4-----5

Total_____

Let My People Grow

KEY CONCEPT TWELVE

Thou shalt not neglect thy newborn children, for they are the fruit of thy labor.

1. As far as knowing the percentage of converts we have retained in the last twelve months

I have no idea	I know the exact percentage

1-----2-----3-----4-----5

2. Our total program for incorporating new converts into the church is

nothing—we have no organized program	well developed highly organized

1-----2-----3-----4-----5

3. Our new convert training class is

nonexistent	continually taught and well attended

1-----2-----3-----4-----5

4. As to helping our new converts develop meaningful friendships among our church family

it's up to new converts to show themselves friendly	we have an organ- ized friendship ministry that's working well

1-----2-----3-----4-----5

5. To encourage new converts to become involved in our church's ministries and programs as soon as possible we

do nothing—it's up to them to show interest or desire for involvement	evaluate monthly to insure that they become involved

1-----2-----3-----4-----5

Total_____

Adding Your Key Concept Score Totals

Take your totals from each page and add them up here.

Totals

KEY CONCEPT ONE   _____

KEY CONCEPT TWO   _____

KEY CONCEPT THREE   _____

KEY CONCEPT FOUR   _____

KEY CONCEPT FIVE   _____

KEY CONCEPT SIX   _____

KEY CONCEPT SEVEN   _____

KEY CONCEPT EIGHT   _____

KEY CONCEPT NINE   _____

KEY CONCEPT TEN   _____

KEY CONCEPT ELEVEN   _____

KEY CONCEPT TWELVE   _____

GRAND TOTAL   _____

Circle the four areas most needing improvement.

Grand Total**	Divide by Twelve	Average
_____	÷ 12 =	_____
	0–4 Poor	
	5–9 Not So Good	_____
Average	10–14 Fair—Average	Final Score
Rating	15–19 Very Good	
	20–25 Excellent	

**Note: Scores may need to be adjusted for church size. If your average attendance is *below fifty,* you do not need a high degree of organization; add twenty-five points to your grand total to allow for this.

Notes

Chapter One
1. For these twelve points, see the Key Concept Evaluation in the appendix.

Chapter Three
1. E. L. Holley, "Managing Your Time Seminar" (Lufkin: Texas District United Pentecostal Church, 1983), p. 20.

2. Frederic Harris Brown, quoted in William H. Cook, *Success, Motivation, and the Scriptures* (Nashville: Broadman Press, 1974), p. 127.

Chapter Four
1. See Olan Hendrix, *Management for the Christian Worker* (Libertyville: Quill Publications, 1975), p. 7.

Chapter Five
1. These are actual results from a church in California after it instituted an annual planning retreat.

2. Proverbs 11:14 (Phillips).

3. These suggestions are given in the management chapter of Tim Massengale, "Total Church Growth" (Fresno, Cal.: Revival Research, 1986). This material comes in two loose-leaf binders with cassettes, and it is available from either the Pentecostal Publishing House or General Home Missions Division of the United Pentecostal Church International.

Chapter Six

1. Recommendations for computers, computer applications, and programs are provided in the evangelism chapter of "Total Church Growth."

2. These suggestions are given in the management chapter of "Total Church Growth."

Chapter Seven

1. This materials list is provided in the leadership development chapter of "Total Church Growth."

2. Brian Tracy, *The Psychology of Achievement* (Chicago: Nightingale-Conant, 1975), tape 2.

3. Adapted from Abraham Maslow's theory of the hierarchy of needs.

4. The sources for these cassette tapes are provided in the leadership development chapter of "Total Church Growth."

Chapter Eight

1. A complete outline of a prayer ministry director's duties is provided in the job descriptions chapter of "Total Church Growth."

2. Richard Heard, "The Climate of Revival," *Let's Have Revival* (Hazelwood, Mo.: General Home Missions Division, UPCI, 1982), pp. 36-38.

Chapter Nine

1. Adapted from E. S. Anderson, *The Sunday School Growth Spiral* (Nashville: Convention Press, 1982), p. 51. For further discussion of the church growth spiral, see "Total Church Growth."

2. The "Fisherman's Workshop" by Al Gossan is

available from the General Home Missions Division, UPCI, or from Pastor Al Gossan in Tampa, Florida.

3. Neil Jackson Jr., *Motivational Ideas for Changing Lives* (Nashville: Broadman Press, 1982), p. 51. For further discussion of Constant Contact Consciousness, see chapter 10 of *Let My People Grow!*

4. Enroll to Grow is an excellent enrollment program available through the General Sunday School Division, UPCI.

Chapter Ten

1. A complete set of church growth spiral worksheets is provided in "Total Church Growth," along with further instruction on implementing this concept successfully.

2. W. A. Criswell, quoted in Larry L. Lewis, *Organize to Evangelize* (Wheaton, Ill.: Victor Books, 1980), p. 27.

3. Adapted from E. S. Anderson, *The Sunday School Growth Spiral.*

Chapter Eleven

1. A complete outline of the New Convert Care System is provided in "Total Church Growth."

2. This card is provided in "Total Church Growth."

3. *Victorious Living for New Christians* (Hazelwood, Mo.: Word Aflame Press, 1970).

4. A sample of this lesson is available from Tim Massengale, Indianapolis, Indiana, for $5.00.

5. This sample letter is provided in "Total Church Growth."

6. W. Charles Arn, "The Friendship Factor," *Church Growth America* (American Institute of Church Growth), May 1981.

7. Al Gossan, "Discipling Believers," *Let's Have Revival,* p. 75.

Chapter Twelve
1. An entire chapter of "Total Church Growth" is devoted to the implementation process.
2. Machiavelli, *The Prince* (1513).
3. Adapted from B. C. Forbes, quoted in Charlie Jones, *Life Is Tremendous!* (Wheaton, Ill.: Tyndale House, 1983), p. 56.

Total Church Growth

Tim Massengale

This outstanding course has been revised and is now contained in two three-ring binders. It also includes the story entitled *Let My People Grow!* which is bound as a separate paperback book. Volume 1 is now entitled *Church Organization and Management;* Volume 2 is entitled *Church Growth and Evangelism.* There are six cassette tapes in this study. Sample forms to assist in organizing, planning, and setting goals for increased church growth are included in these two volumes. This dynamic course is having tremendous results among our fellowship.

Please send me:

Qty.   Amount

____ (9095111366) Total Church Growth $69.95 _____

____ (1412) Let My People Grow $7.99 . . . . . . _____

Missouri Residents Add 5.975% Sales Tax _____

12% Postage & Handling (Minimum $1.00) _____

Canadian Postage 20% (Minimum $1.50) _____
Pay in US Funds

Foreign Postage 30% (Minimum $1.50) _____

Total _____

Customer # _____

VISA   MasterCard   DISCOVER

Charge my:
☐ VISA ☐ MasterCard ☐ DISCOVER
Credit Card No.

MasterCard Interbank No. | | | |
(above your name)

Expiration Date Mo. _____ Year _____

_____
Signature as it appears on credit card

Name _____

Address _____

City _____

State_____ Zip_____

Phone _____

Order from: Word Aflame Press
8855 Dunn Road
Hazelwood, MO 63042-2299
Phone: 314-837-7300